Language Learning Laughs

Language and Cultural Bloopers & Stories From
Around the World

Marci Renée

The Cultural Story-Weaver

Copyright © 2021 by Marci Renée

All rights reserved. Published by The Cultural Story-Weaver.

No part of this publication may be reproduced in whole or in part, or stored in a retrieval system, or transmitted in any form or by any means, electronic, mechanical, photocopying, recording, or otherwise, without written permission of the publisher. For information regarding permission, contact The Cultural Story-Weaver at www.culturalstoryweaver.com.

ISBN 978-1-7367253-6-8

I dedicate this book to Ann, my first and favorite French teacher. Thank you for sharing your love and passion for language and culture with me. Your "foreign language fever" was contagious! Thank you to my mother, who encouraged me to follow my dreams and released me to live the rest of my life on the other side of the ocean at the age of nineteen. Thank you to my husband and four sons, who have labored alongside me to learn foreign languages and cultures around the globe. You have demonstrated great courage and dedication in building bridges to the world. It's been fun—with much laughter and tears!

"Traveling—it leaves you speechless, then turns you into a storyteller."

—Ibn Battuta

Contents

It Started With a Bonjour!

"Oh, the places you'll go!"

—Dr. Seuss

I can still remember the moment. I can still feel the emotion. I can still see the classroom, sitting there on the floor, Indian-style, with bright eyes and eager expectation. Only nine-years-old, wearing long ponytails, my heart beating fast.

Breath blew into me with that one simple word, "Bonjour!"

Something came alive in me when I first heard that beautiful language. It was as if something was birthed inside my heart . . . or perhaps something was awakened deep within my soul . . . something lying dormant.

At that moment, I fell in love—not love at first sight—but love at first sound. "Bonjour." I felt its rhythm, its song, its accent ripple throughout my body.

"Bonjour." I heard my destiny calling me. That one brief word invited me, beckoned me to come.

I ran home from school that afternoon.

"I'm going to live in France one day!" I screamed eagerly as my mother barreled through the door after a long, hard day at work.

She was confused, but I was not. My mind was clear . . . determined. I knew exactly where I was going and what I wanted to do. I caught my dream that day, and I never let it go.

Never.

Ten years later, at age nineteen, I boarded an airplane in my hometown in Missouri, in the middle of America, to fly to the other side of the ocean.

My French dream awaited me. The love of my life would greet me at the border. I was not disappointed. I felt her loving arms wrap around me . . . welcome me. My passion and love grew with every moment, every sight, every sound, every taste, every person, every experience.

Cobblestone roads, red geraniums in window boxes, freshly baked baguettes, plaid berets, piles of warm crêpes heaping with chocolate, blooming irises of every color of the rainbow, a charming Frenchman who would one day become my husband and the father of my four children. It was no longer a childhood dream; it was my life—my reality.

Since that first day of stepping foot on your soil, I have traveled to more than thirty countries and lived in many foreign lands.

But, my dear France, you will always be my first love. My dear France, you will always be my beloved. It only took that one little word, "Bonjour," and you captured my heart . . . forever.

Language Learning Can Be Fun?

"To learn a new language is, therefore, always a sort of spiritual adventure; it is like a journey of discovery in which we find a new world." – Ernst Cassirer

I have loved languages since I was nine. That's how old I was when I first heard a foreign language, one different than the one I grew up speaking.

Before that, I am not sure if I knew that foreign countries, cultures, and languages existed. I was a Missouri girl, born and immersed in the English language, born and raised in deep Midwestern culture.

I didn't know any different. It was innate. It was natural. It was deeply ingrained in me.

The day I heard French for the first time, the day I heard a new language, I had a radical paradigm shift.

I realized there was a great big world out there, full of people who were different from me. For the first time in my life, I was confronted with the awesome reality that there were people who looked differently than me, talked differently than me, dressed differently than me, learned differently from me, thought differently from me, and lived differently than me. And there were people around the world who ate things other than cheeseburgers, french fries, fried chicken, Grandma Esther's Creamed Corn Casserole, Grandpa Al's fried crappie, and pumpkin pie.

Sitting in my fourth-grade classroom each week for French class, I fell in love with languages and the intricacies of words, accents, structures, and sounds. Life suddenly became a word puzzle for me to look at, to admire, to study, and to put together. I became fascinated with language rhythm. It was like music to my ears. I could hear words sing and dance, and it made me happy.

A decade later, while sitting in one of my university French classes, I came across a quote by a famous French philosopher, Montesquieu.

"Teaching is learning twice."

At that moment, I knew I loved languages, and I knew I wanted to teach languages—my language, foreign languages, any language. It didn't matter, but I knew I would forever be a student of language and a teacher of language. I wanted everyone to fall in love with foreign languages—just like me!

I quickly discovered that a language is a bridge to the world. It's a bridge to travel, a bridge to have a conversation with someone from a foreign land, a bridge to deep cultural awareness and learning.

Yes, a language is a bridge to the world!

At the age of twelve, I jumped at the opportunity to continue studying French at my junior high school. I couldn't get enough of it. Only one hour a day—you have to be kidding me! I wanted to study the French language and culture all day, every day of the week.

I enjoyed it, but I soon realized that my classmates didn't all have the same passion and perspective as I did. Many of the students complained about not understanding. Some were frustrated for "not getting it." Others saw no value, no use, no practical reason to study French. I mean, really, we lived in Missouri. What were the chances that we would actually meet a French person and have an opportunity to say, "*Bonjour! Ça va?*"

It didn't matter what others said about French and foreign languages, nothing was going to sway me or change my mind. I loved languages!

Why? Why was my experience with learning a foreign language different from the student sitting next to me?

Ok, let's be honest, learning language comes more easily for some than others. There is an assessment called the MLAT, Modern Language Aptitude Test. It's required by many companies and organizations who send people overseas to live and work, often requiring the study and mastery of the local language.

Before moving to Morocco to work with our organization, my husband and I had to take the MLAT. I actually liked taking it and scored well; however, that wasn't the case for everyone. Based on one's score, the organization could then determine if the person should be placed in a country with a language that is difficult to learn, like Arabic or Mandarin, or in a country with a language that is easier to learn, like Spanish.

All that to say, I can't discount the reality that not everyone learns languages quickly and easily. I was also a foreign language teacher when we first moved to Morocco to learn Arabic. Certified to teach French to children from kindergarten to the twelfth grade, I had an obvious passion and knack for languages.

Yes, all these things certainly helped me enjoy the intensive, and at times, grueling, act of language learning. However, I'm convinced that there was something else that helped me even more than my ability or my fascination with language. It still helps me today, as I now immerse myself in a new (fourth!) language and culture in Spain.

Hopefully, by now, you are asking, "What?! What helped?! What was it?!"

You might be surprised, but it's actually quite simple, and everyone can access it. It's a language learning tool that is free and readily available. The item never goes out of stock. There is an abundant supply worldwide. It's actually so ridiculously easy and obvious that we overlook it.

LAUGHTER!

One of the first things I learned to do with learning a foreign language was to laugh at myself and to laugh with others. Of all things you can have fun learning, foreign languages rank top on the list!

I'm always disappointed to hear of children and adults who hate learning languages, because their English or French or Spanish teacher is boring and purely academic. I've also talked to many—adults and children alike—who are terrified to open their mouths in a foreign language classroom. They fear sounding silly, stupid, or making mistakes.

While living in France and teaching English to Airbus professionals, I was shocked to hear their stories of learning English. They were constantly corrected and had little freedom to open their mouths, try to communicate, and make mistakes. In that type of learning environment, I would hate languages too.

So, who said that language learning has to be hard and boring? It honestly can be boatloads of fun! If you take French or English with me in the classroom, you will usually leave with a bellyache! We laugh, we joke, we dance, we sing, we make faces, we act silly . . .

WE LAUGH!!!

And, I'm not just talking about 5-year-olds. Those Airbus professionals, all decked out in suits and ties, had no idea that learning English could be so much fun! They often expressed that they learned more in my English classes than they did in all their years combined in English classes at school.

Why? What was the difference?

WE LAUGHED!

I believe that laughter, fun, and humor in language learning is one of the essential keys to success. Laughter relaxes the body, relaxes the mind, relaxes the atmosphere, and as a result, we are more at ease and more apt to absorb new concepts. Our brains are better prepared to pave new neural pathways of learning.

As a teacher of foreign languages, I laugh, and as a student of foreign languages, I laugh.

Whether it be in France, in Morocco, or now in Spain, I laugh while learning languages. I laugh A LOT!

During our seven years living in Morocco, I can recall going to *hanoutes*—local corner grocery stores—markets, schools, and neighbors' homes, where I would need to speak Arabic. With my imperfect grammar, broken sentence structure, lack of correct vocabulary, and my strong American accent, almost always, people would smile and often laugh.

At that moment, I had a choice. I could get irritated, defensive, and mad . . . or . . . I could laugh! I tried to always choose the latter. Instead of getting upset, angry, frustrated, or offended, I always said the same thing . . .

"Are you laughing AT me?!"

Then I would smile and chuckle.

The person in front of me would always respond with the same words and same embarrassed, turned-down gaze.

"No, of course, I'm not laughing at you!"

I would then say, "No, you aren't laughing AT me, you are laughing WITH me! And, I'm laughing too!"

This brief conversation opened doors of friendship, built bridges between our foreign worlds, and brought us fun, laughter, and smiles.

Today, I invite you on this journey of laughter in language learning. It's my personal journey, but it represents the many others around the world who spend countless hours, days, weeks, months, and years learning foreign languages. We all do this to build bridges, bridges to the world. This is noble and honorable. I applaud us all for our hard work and effort. It is extremely hard work!

However, let's not forget one of the essential keys to unlocking success in language learning—LAUGHTER! Let us not forget to laugh at ourselves and with others. It's amazing how that slight shift in perspective can change everything and can actually make us better language learners.

For the rest of the world, I hope these funny stories of our family's language and culture bloopers around the world will entertain you and will encourage you all to jump on the language learning bandwagon. It's a fun and wild ride you won't want to miss! It's actually not a bandwagon, it's a camel. Yes, it will be bumpy and terrifying on the high dunes, your bum and legs will be sore beyond words the next day, and you may fall off onto the hard sand (like I did in Morocco). But, if you keep laughing at yourself and keep laughing with others, you will build a bridge to the world . . . and fall in love with it at the same time.

So, jump on the camel's back! But hold on tight to the reins. As the camel slowly stands up, you will be violently jerked forwards and backwards!

WARNING! BEWARE OF LAUGHTER, TEARS, AND A BELLYACHE!

WARNING! PART 5 CONTAINS SOME "UNINTENTIONAL VULGARITY"! HA! THIS SECTION IS NOT INTENDED FOR YOUNGER READERS.

Part 1

Hilarious Kid Humor

Chapter One
How to Horrify Your New Babysitter!

"Own only what you can always carry with you:
know languages, know countries, know people.
Let your memory be your travel bag." –
Aleksandr Solzhenitsyn

When we first arrived in Morocco years ago, our boys (We only had two at the time!) were five and three. We were just beginning to learn Arabic.

Fatima, a wonderful local woman, had just started helping us with childcare. My husband and I needed to go to the grocery store, and we wanted to explain to the babysitter that we would be gone for two hours.

Hard Work and Courage

I worked hard to formulate and practice my sentences in my new language. It took me even more time to muster up enough courage to approach Fatima, open my mouth, and try to pronounce it correctly.

"Fatima, we are going to the grocery store, and we are leaving the two boys with you. We will only be gone for two YEARS."

I saw the look of surprise and horror on her face, and I knew immediately that I had said something wrong. Fatima then began chuckling, and I had no idea why. I just knew that whatever I had said was very funny.

"Two years?!" she said in between timid giggles.

Laughing at Myself

It took me a while to realize what I had said. But, as soon as I did, I began laughing too. The Arabic word for "two years" is close to the word for "two hours," or at least similar enough for a new Arabic language learner—like me— to mix up. In all honesty, the only real similarity is that both words begin with the "s" sound!

Fatima was relieved to know that we would not abandon our two boys with her for two years—after just arriving in a new country! My limited Arabic obviously didn't allow me to give her any more instructions for the kids. Thankfully, Fatima was amazing and could interpret my gestures, drawings, facial expressions, etc. She knew she would be fine with our boys for just "two hours"!

Let's Weave Cultures!

How do you keep a humble attitude while learning a new language and culture? How do you respond when people laugh at you when you are learning a foreign language?

Chapter Two

Culturally Appropriate? 'Al-hamdu-li-llāh!'

R aising kids "across cultures" can be fun, challenging, and yes, even confusing . . . for them and for us!

When our boys (only three of them at the time!) were nine, seven, and two, we returned to the United States to spend the summer months with my American family. During that time, they enjoyed spending time with their long-lost cousins who enjoyed fishing, running around barefoot, playing with chickens, and belching loudly in public!

Our boys quickly picked up the exciting habit of burping out loud. Well, exciting for them—not for me! They failed to forget that their father, being French, was much more "proper" in his bodily functions and found the less-than-discreet sounds emanating from his children's mouths to be quite shocking and offensive. This was contrary to the way French children were to behave! In our home, or in public with us, we continually reminded our children that this behavior was inappropriate . . . much to their dismay.

If a burp slipped out unexpectedly and audibly, we would gently nudge them in their recollection by asking, "What do you say?" They would typically respond with the culturally appropriate, "Excuse me" or "*Excusez-moi*," depending on who they were speaking to . . . Mom or Dad.

But, culturally appropriate WHERE?

Shortly after our return to our home in Morocco at the end of summer vacation, we were invited one afternoon to visit our local friends for mint tea and cookies. I would typically bring the boys along on my visits. They loved to drink mint tea, "*etay*," (sometimes the entire teapot!) and to savor the delicious local treats of warm Moroccan crêpes called *"m'simmons,"* lathered with melted honey and butter.

Timothée, our oldest son, was nine. After playing outside in the dirt street with the other Moroccan children, he came inside my friend's small village house to devour some freshly made *crêpes* and to gulp down multiple glasses of hot, sweet mint tea. After washing down the last bite, he opened his mouth. Much to my horror, a very loud, rolling, eternal, boisterous burp erupted from the pit of his stomach! I almost had a heart attack as my mind and heart swelled with embarrassment and disbelief.

Quickly turning to my impolite and uneducated child, my eyes were wide open and my eyebrows raised to the ceiling of my forehead. With a more than stern voice, I said, "Timothée, what do you say?" I don't even recall which language I used to ask my question. Was it English? French? Arabic? In any case, my son understood me, and he knew exactly how to respond . . .

"Al-hamdu-li-llah!" (Arabic: الْحَمْدُ للهِ)

In response to Timothée, my Moroccan friend, Ghadouge, echoed loudly, *"Al-hamdu-li-llah,"* meaning "Praise be to God!"

I was suddenly shaken awake to the reality that I was no longer in my American or French cultural context, but I was back "home" in my Arab environment . . . the culture and land where Timothée and our other children had been raised during some of their most formative years. Of course, my son would verbally express praise and thanksgiving for the food and drink that he had just enjoyed in the home of our local hosts. It was absolutely culturally appropriate!

Arab culture was rich in hospitality and had mastered its art. Our Moroccan friends, even those who could not afford to eat meat, would generously give of everything they had to honor the guests who would walk through their door.

It was the greatest honor of the cook if his or her guests would express their love and appreciation for the meal by a loud belch, followed by the verbal expression of *"Al-hamdu-li-llah!"* And don't just think that the men do it. The women actually seem to have louder and deeper belches than the men. My mind will never let me forget the first time I heard my sweet, elderly, petite Moroccan friend "let it rip!" I tried hard to remain calm and collected, in between my overwhelming feelings of shock and disgust.

After the belch, the instigator must proudly proclaim "*Al-hamdu-li-llah.*" In return, others within hearing will echo his or her praises to God, by replying "*Al-hamdu-li-llah!*" The Arab cook could actually be offended if no one offers praises to God through this culturally appropriate expression! It is truly music to their ears and represents great honor.

Following Ghadouge's reply of "*Al-hamdu-li-llah,*" Timothée turned to me and grinned mischievously. He knew I was trapped. I replied, "*Al-hamdu-li-llah,*" and we all chuckled.

Ghadouge was delighted, and so was Timothée. I, on the other hand, was already planning in my mind the discussion that I would have with my son about cultural inappropriateness.

But once again, were my kids American? French? Moroccan?

Their home was in Morocco, so they probably felt more Moroccan than anything else. What could I expect? My son was actually being culturally appropriate.

In this story, along with all the others, I have had to remind myself and my children that . . . it's not good, it's not bad, it's not better, it's not worse . . . it's just different!

Raising kids "across cultures" can be fun, challenging, and yes, even very confusing . . . for them and for us! Thankfully, this confusion leads to great learning that can help us all become more-informed, global travelers and greater global citizens in our world. This learning breaks down cultural barriers between us and bridges our worlds.

Let's Weave Cultures!

What are some things you find strange, and perhaps even offensive, in other cultures . . . even though they are entirely appropriate in that culture?

Chapter Three
Crossing Borders = Crossing Currencies

"Learning a new language is becoming a
member of the club – the community of speakers
of that language." – Frank Smith

"Do they use the same 'George Washington money' in Florida as they do in Pennsylvania?"

I was cooking dinner, while my 8-year-old son, Pierre, scrambled through his long-lost billfold found in the drawer of his bedroom dresser. The faded Barcelona emblem, and the broken zipper showed its love and extensive use. It was actually a hand-me-down from one of his three older brothers.

He counted the six wrinkled, faded bills joyfully, already dreaming of his next purchases.

Pierre lives "across borders, across cultures, and across languages." Born in France, lived in the United States, Pierre now lives in Spain. In his brief life, he has traveled to more countries than he can count on his two little hands. Across borders . . . and often, across currencies. Pierre knows all about money conversion—exchanging money. He knows about *dollars, euros, dirhams, CFA francs, pesos . . .*

Did you know there are 180 different currencies in the world? [1]

Money Exchange

Living in Spain, Pierre often heard us talking about the exchange rate between euros and dollars. Money conversion is a part of our world, a part of our life. When you cross borders, you exchange money. No two lands on different sides of a border could possibly use the same money, the same currency, the same "George Washington bills." At least, that's what Pierre thought.

Pierre lived in Pennsylvania for 1 1/2 years, between the ages of four and six. He was excited to return there to visit his friends this summer. He also knew we were going to cross state borders. Nana lives in Missouri, but Grandma, Grandpa, Aunt Kimi, Uncle Parker, and his cousins live in Florida. He knew he was going to be crossing borders, and he assumed that also meant crossing currencies.

"Do they use the same 'George Washington money' in Florida as they do in Pennsylvania?" Pierre asked.

"They sure do!" I replied. "Makes for easy travel and no loss on the foreign exchange!"

U.S.A . . . here we come . . . carrying our "George Washington money"!

Let's Weave Cultures!

What is your experience of crossing borders and crossing currencies? Do you find exchanging currencies to be challenging?

{1} Travelex.com https://www.travelex.com/currency/current-world-currencies

Chapter Four

Hunting for Easter Eggs Around the World

T his year, in our new home in Spain, I don't have any colored egg dye. I've also learned from experience that European brown eggs don't dye as well as white American eggs! I also don't have any bright-colored plastic eggs to fill or chocolate eggs to hide in the garden.

Perhaps that's not a bad thing. It allows us to keep our eyes on the true meaning of Easter—the death and resurrection of Jesus.

During our global crisis, I hope this Easter egg story can make you laugh and brighten up your day. We can all use that right now.

It's also interesting to see the different Easter traditions in the U.S. and in France. So, put on your cultural awareness glasses!

Remembering . . . A Few Years Ago

April 22, 2019

It was my youngest son's first official "Easter egg hunt." America seems to be the only place where you can experience these public cultural events in the local community. In France and Morocco, I always managed to find some foil-covered, miniature chocolate eggs to hide around the house or the yard. If we couldn't find them in a store somewhere, I would often have some friends or family bring them over from the U.S. Another option was filling our large, bright-colored, plastic eggs that we had collected over the years with little local treats.

Hunting for Hard-Boiled Eggs

Every year in Morocco, I can remember going to the forest with several families after Easter service at church for a picnic and an Easter Egg hunt—with real, color-dyed, hard-boiled eggs. The hunt was fun for the kids, but the adults were the only ones who would enjoy eating the eggs.

Of our four boys, I can only recall Timothée having an opportunity for a "real" Easter Egg hunt in America—with lots of kids running around, racing for the colorful egg prizes lying in the grass. I had deprived my other boys of this American cultural experience—among many others!

His First Easter Egg Hunt!

A local friend in Pennsylvania told me to check out the town's Easter egg hunt, so off my son, Pierre, and I went. She warned me, "Get there early! They start on time, and it goes by quickly!" Pierre was so excited! We arrived just a few minutes before the starting time. There were many people, so we went to the nearest opening in the crowd. While waiting on the sideline with all the other children, I gave Pierre instructions. The bell rang, and off the kids went!

I watched as Pierre scrambled and rounded up the plastic eggs in his cloth grocery bag. He seemed to beat all the little kids, which made me feel guilty. He looked so big out there! Maybe he should leave some behind for the toddlers crawling on the ground, hoping to grab one little prize. Pierre ended up with an entire bag full of plastic eggs. In a matter of sixty seconds, the hunt was over! It was truly the fastest race I had ever seen.

Disappointment

Pierre, along with all the other children, frantically began opening their plastic eggs. There wasn't much in them—just a few cheap plastic toys. The loot was disappointing.

Suddenly, Pierre and I noticed some "older" children—about his age—opening their eggs. They were filled with cool candy and fun prizes.

"That's strange," I thought to myself.

Oops!

I then noticed a large sign next to the grassy lawn where we were standing. It said, "0-3 years." As the crowd cleared, I noticed the signs in the other grassy areas off in the near distance, "4-6 years" and "7 years plus." As a six-year-old, Pierre had obviously been in the wrong age group.

I explained it to Pierre, and he said, "Mommy, you didn't know how to do it."

I apologized and said to my disappointed child, "I'm sorry. You're right, Mommy didn't know how to do it. This is my first time in about twenty years that I've been to a real Easter egg hunt."

We walked to the car laughing, then we drove to the dollar store to buy a bag of foil-covered chocolate eggs to hide in the house. That is much easier, and we won't be stealing all the babies' Easter eggs!

Easter *"Pâques"* in France

"Easter," *"Pâques,"* in French means "Passover."

In the U.S., the "Easter Bunny" traditionally delivers and hides the Easter eggs. When I tried to explain that to my children, I could not answer their curious questions about bunnies and eggs. Why not have an "Easter Chicken"?

In France, it's not the "Easter Bunny," but the "Flying Easter Bells" who bring the eggs to children on Easter morning. That doesn't seem to make any more sense than the "Easter Bunny."

I have to continually remind myself and my children . . . it's not good, it's not bad, it's not better, it's not worse . . . it's just different!

"The Catholic tradition dictates that church bells don't ring between Good Friday, *'Vendredi Saint,'* and Easter Sunday, to commemorate the death of Christ and his resurrection. The oral tradition then said that the bells were flying to Rome during that time (they then grow two little wings and dress up with a lovely ribbon) to be blessed by the Pope, and then come back from this trip loaded with presents." (French Today*)

Because of the "Flying Easter Bells," "*Les Cloches de Pâques,*" one will typically give gifts of chocolate "bells," rather than chocolate "bunnies." Also, one will often see chocolate "hens" in France. Now, that makes sense!

The French also don't eat the traditional American "Easter ham" for their Easter meal. Rather, they celebrate with omelets or a leg of lamb—representing the traditional "Passover Lamb."

In the town of Bessières, "a steel fry pan four meters in diameter and weighing a ton is installed with a crane onto a bed of hot coals. The handle of the fry pan is simply a wooden pole. The quantity of ingredients is impressive: 15,000 eggs, twenty-five liters of oil, six kilos of seasoning, dozens of bunches of chives, hand chopped. It also takes a lot of elbow grease to prepare all that in time . . . and we don't make an omelette without breaking any eggs . . . When all the eggs are beaten and poured into the gigantic fry pan, a dozen cooks armed with large wooden spoons stir the mixture." (The Local*) The giant omelette is then cut and served to all who have come.

Now, that's what I call a giant omelette and a community Easter meal!

Let's Weave Cultures!

How do you celebrate Easter in your country? What are your cultural traditions?

*https://www.frenchtoday.com/blog/french-culture/french-traditions-easter-egg-lamb-meal-traditional/

*https://www.thelocal.fr/20190415/6-ways-the-french-celebrate-easter/

Chapter Five
˚What's Wrong With This Picture?˚

"To learn a language is to have one more
window from which to look at the world." –
Chinese Proverb

It was Thanksgiving Eve, and we were doing some grocery shopping.

Pierre, my seven-year-old son, was thrilled to see the display of chocolate Advent calendars, the ones with the little windows you open each day from December 1 to December 25. Each door reveals a cute little chocolate surprise for each day.

"Advent" means "Before" . . . it's the preparation of Christmas, the countdown to the coming of Jesus. It's a time, not just to eat delicious chocolate, but a time to prepare our hearts and to remind ourselves and others what the true meaning of Christmas is.

I told Pierre that he could choose one of two designs—the cheaper chocolate Advent calendar versions. We quickly skimmed over the fancy Star Wars ones, the expensive Lindt chocolate ones, etc. Yes, this miserly mother was willing to pay ninety-nine centimes, but not eight euros!

Pierre quickly chose one that had three kings on it—the three wise men who brought gifts to Jesus after His birth. It was nice.

"Great!" I told him. "Do you want to pick one out for David and Timothée too?" He chose the other version for them.

When we got home, Pierre looked strangely at his "Three Kings" calendar.

"It's missing the seven," he said.

That's so strange, I thought to myself. Why would it be missing the seven? What's wrong with this calendar?

My husband and I looked at it, curiously trying to find the reason for the counting error.

Finally, I saw the "*dec*" written underneath some numbers, and the "*ene*" written under the others.

"It's a King's Day calendar, not an Advent calendar!" I said. "That's why there's no seven! It ends on January 6—'Kings' Day' in Spain!"

"*Dec*" was for December, and "*ene*" was for January in Spanish.

We looked at the chocolate calendar closely. It didn't start on December 1. It began on December 14 and ended on January 6—"Kings' Day"!

In Spanish culture, children rarely get their gifts on Christmas morning like in many parts of the world. Rather, they have to wait until January 6 when the "Three Kings" give their gifts to Baby Jesus. That is the day of gift giving in Spain!

Of course they have a Kings' Calendar on the Spanish grocery shelves, right alongside the Christmas Advent calendars for kids like Pierre from the other side of the world. We are clearly strangers in this foreign land!

Now, at Christmastime, in our home in Spain, we have two different cultures, two different traditions sitting side by side—the Christmas advent calendar and the Three Kings' calendar. We can begin opening the little windows of one of them on December 1. The other one has to wait patiently to be opened on December 14!

So, what's wrong with this picture!?

Absolutely nothing! It's not good or bad, right or wrong, better or worse ...
it's just different!

Let's Weave Cultures!

**How do you celebrate Advent in your country? What are your cultural
traditions?**

Part 2

Language Laughter

Chapter Six

I Learned Spanish in Zumba Class

What is the best way to learn a foreign language?

While living in the U.S., one activity that I enjoyed doing weekly at the local gym was Zumba. It has fun dancing and music, and it's another great way to meet women in the community. If you have ever done Zumba, you know that the music and dance are from Latin America and most of the music is in Spanish.

"Zumba Spanish," as I call it!

When living in southwestern France, Spain was our family's favorite vacation spot. In about forty-five minutes, we could cross the border into Spain and suddenly find ourselves in an entirely different world. We were immediately immersed in a different country, different language, and different culture. The people looked and acted differently, and the Spanish food and lifestyle were worlds apart from the French. *Paella, tortilla* omelettes, *tapas*, and fresh *churros* dipped in hot chocolate were on every street corner.

We also loved the relaxed rhythm of life, with late breakfasts around 10 a.m., late lunches around 2 p.m, followed by afternoon *siestas*. Late dinners ended the day around 10 p.m. It may not be a time schedule that suits everyone, but our family had no problem adapting.

The language, however, was another story. At the time, we were very limited in our Spanish, squeezing by with only a handful of practical phrases, like *"hola"* and *"cómo estás."* The expression that always came in handy was the usual, *"No hablo español."* ("I don't speak Spanish.") We hoped the listener would be especially gracious and kind to us in knowing that we didn't speak a word of Spanish. They were usually, however, touched because we at least tried to speak a few words of their language.

One morning, during my Zumba class, I realized I had really progressed in my Spanish-speaking abilities. After months of hearing "Zumba Spanish" one hour per week, my vocabulary had increased significantly.

"Checking out" of my Zumba class mentally, I suddenly imagined myself walking the streets of Barcelona.

I could hear myself saying, *"Bella, Pedro, el Zumba, Roberto, bonito, mucho, despacito . . ."* while trying to order in a local restaurant. I realized that "Zumba Spanish" was actually quite limiting. Honestly, my ignorance hindered me from really knowing what I was saying. As I stumbled over my own two feet, missing multiple dance steps, I quickly snapped out of my Spanish dream. The hard reality hit me that I was in a gym studio in rural Pennsylvania . . . not exotic cobble-stoned European alleys.

I began chuckling to myself as I recalled the many times I had used vocabulary or expressions in new languages, not fully grasping the meaning behind the words.

Many silly mistakes, sometimes even offensive ones, have blurted out of my mouth! As I reminisced, I actually began laughing out loud while doing my Zumba dance moves. I'm not sure what my Zumba instructor was thinking about me, other than that I was really enjoying her class.

I recall all too vividly my first major contextual mistake in my French language learning. My first summer days in France were spent with a three-year-old, reading children's stories, or with my boyfriend, Vincent, and his "gang" of friends, going to local restaurants and *discothèques*.

My French was improving rapidly. I was picking up all kinds of slang and "cuss" words, even though I didn't realize it. When you learn a new language, it's hard to pick up on all the cultural and contextual nuances behind the words. As a good language learner, I just proudly repeated and practiced my new vocabulary and grammatical structures.

One evening, shortly after being introduced to Vincent's parents, I was invited by them to a fancy, creole restaurant for dinner. It was a huge celebration with their friends, and everyone was enjoying drinking the local rum. Vincent's mother, Sylvette, was dancing and having a good time. She was really enjoying the rum!

I was dancing next to her and yelled over the music, "*Tu es bourrée!*" and laughed. I THOUGHT I was kindly remarking that she had been drinking a little too much. However, I could read the shock on her face, as well as on the faces of her friends who were dancing with us. My intent had clearly not been communicated.

One of her friends explained to me that my word choice was very vulgar and offensive.

Oh my goodness, I had just insulted my future mother-in-law and didn't even realize it!

I had been learning all kinds of words and expressions from Vincent and his friends during those summer months. However, I had not learned in which contexts to use the words and expressions. I learned my lesson that day. One must learn context and culture alongside any language. It's all a part of language learning.

I apologized profusely for offending Vincent's mother and for using words and expressions ignorantly.

Thankfully, people are usually forgiving of the foreigner who is trying to learn their beautiful language and massacring it in the process.

It's all because of ignorance. My intention is never, by any means, to offend my cultural hosts. Sometimes, I just communicate things and have no idea what I'm saying . . . kinda like with "Zumba Spanish!"

It reminds me of others I have seen making similar mistakes, all in ignorance and naivety. For example, one will sometimes pass people in faraway lands in Africa or Asia who are wearing shirts with American cuss words or other shocking expressions on them. They are communicating messages through their clothes, and they have no idea what they are wearing . . . and saying!

Other times, I have heard young French or Korean teenagers singing the lyrics of their favorite American music. They have memorized these songs word for word. They belt out the words. Yet, they have absolutely no idea what they are communicating. This can be quite dangerous!

We must be on guard with what we are communicating in new foreign languages, through our verbal messages, through music lyrics, and through our clothing messages.

We must also study and ask good questions to better understand the cultural context in which we are living and interacting. If not, the language and cultural bridges that we are attempting to build with our cultural hosts may crumble under the weight of vulgarity and offense.

One way to do this is to ask native speakers questions when learning unfamiliar words and expressions. For example, "In what context would you use this word or expression?" or "What type of people can I use this expression with?"

Don't let this scare you and keep you from going out there and learning a new language! We all have lessons to learn.

Let's Weave Cultures!

What "unknown" or "unseen" messages have you accidentally communicated in foreign languages and cultures? What messages do you see those around you communicating in their cultural and linguistic ignorance?

Chapter Seven

10 Words in England You May Not Understand

"To learn a new language is, therefore, always a sort of spiritual adventure; it is like a journey of discovery in which we find a new world." – Ernst Cassirer

Perhaps you are an American, and you have never traveled to the United Kingdom (U.K.). Or perhaps you have never had the privilege of being around British citizens. If that's the case, you may not know that American English and British English are two very different languages. Yes, the accent is extremely different, but there are also some major differences in expressions and vocabulary. While traveling in England recently to visit my son at the university , I was reminded of this reality.

10 Common British Words

I have traveled to England before, and I have a lot of British friends. Therefore, I am familiar with these words and know their meanings. However, if it's your first trip to England, you may not understand these words. This can lead to some real confusion. Here are ten common British words and their meanings:

—Cheers = thank you or goodbye

—Love = the equivalent to "Dear" in American English. Perfect strangers will call you "Love." For example, "Let me help you with the door, Love." It can be shocking at first, because it seems that the man or woman is flirting with you!

—Mate = friend

—Tap = the word used for faucet. The waitress at the restaurant may ask you if you would like some "tap water."

—Rubber = a pencil eraser—not a condom

—Bits and bobs = odds and ends

—Gents = short for gentlemen. You will see this on the sign for the men's restroom.

—Lift = elevator

—Bloody = a swear word used to emphasize something. For example, "That was a bloody good football game!"

—Loo = restroom or toilet

Believe me, there are more than ten confusing British English words. However, this will get you started on your next trip to the United Kingdom!

Let's Weave Cultures!

Have you traveled to England or another English-speaking country? What are some of the different vocabulary or expressions?

Chapter Eight
Eating Humble Pie

"**A**re you laughing at me?" I would often ask my Moroccan friends and neighbors while living in North Africa.

It didn't just happen with people I knew, it happened with complete strangers in the corner *"hanoute"* grocery store, the outdoor market, the doctor's office, the public school . . . everywhere.

"Are you laughing at me?"

"No, I'm not laughing at you. I'm laughing with you," they would usually respond.

With only a slight preposition change in the Arabic language, the meaning changed significantly.

"At least I bring a smile to your face and some laughter in the air!" I always replied.

It's difficult to have someone laugh when you are struggling to speak a foreign language. Whether they are laughing AT you, WITH you, or any other way, it's embarrassing. It's humbling. When learning a foreign language, you often eat "humble pie."

Struggling

No longer struggling with Arabic, I now struggle with a new language—Spanish. I would like to say that I'm fluent after living in-country for two years, but I'm not. I'm far from it. This week, once again, I struggled to communicate—struggled to express what I wanted and needed to say, struggled to be understood.

It seems like making appointments for my son's allergy shots at the public health center would be easy. Right? Wrong!

Some people aren't used to hearing foreign accents, so their ears and brains tell them—from the first word, the first hint of accent—"I don't understand you. I don't want to understand you. I don't want to try to understand you. Go away. Go back to your country."

Others don't have the time or patience to understand. This was clearly the case of the woman wearing strict eyeglasses, behind the plexiglass window, at the health center that day.

After a few moments of back-and-forth leaps over the very obvious barriers between us, the language and "THE MASK," the woman in front of me turned to her colleague and said, "*Su español es fatal!*" (translation: "Her Spanish is a disaster—dead, fatal, mortal, lethal, lifeless!")

I heard. I understood.

My first response was to chuckle and brush it off. "*Si, si, mi español es muy fatal!*" (Yes, yes, my Spanish is a very dead!)

However, deep inside, I could feel the frustration, the embarrassment, the anger rise.

I Wanted to Scream!

I wanted to scream . . . "At least I'm here in Spain, trying to learn your language. At least I'm trying and not using Google Translate as a crutch. What about you? How many languages do you speak, lady? One? Spanish? Well, I speak four languages! Ok, the fourth one might not be at an advanced level, but at least I'm trying!"

Instead, I prayed for an extra dose of kindness and patience . . . and humility. I nodded at the two women and smiled.

The next time they asked me a question, I quickly pulled out my phone to find my good, 'ole trusted friend, Google Translate. If SHE (Yes, Google Translate must surely be an outrageously intelligent woman who speaks all the languages of the world fluently!) made a mistake, at least these women's irritability, mockery, and impatience would be directed at my held-up phone screen and not at my face.

Thankfully, God gave me the self-control and discipline to keep my mouth shut that day. Well, not completely. I opened up my mouth just enough for these women to serve me a nice, gigantic piece of "humble pie"!

Yummy! I think this one was cherry!

Let's Weave Cultures!

Have you ever learned a foreign language? What were some challenges you faced? If people laughed at you, what was that experience like? How did you digest your "humble pie"?

Chapter Nine

Do You Want Paper or Plastic?

"To have another language is to possess a second soul." —Charlemagne

My husband's first trip to the grocery store in America is one that will remain etched forever in our memory.

When checking out, the cashier asked Vincent, "Do you want paper or plastic?"

Vincent pulled out his wallet from his jeans. He handed the cashier a twenty-dollar bill and told her he would like to pay with "paper" money rather than a "plastic" credit card.

The cashier looked confused.

In French, I explained to Vincent that the cashier was not referring to his method of payment, but she was asking if he wanted his groceries sacked in "plastic" bags or brown "paper" bags.

We all laughed together!

I wonder if that cashier in Missouri still remembers that funny linguistic and cultural incident as clearly as we do?!

Let's Weave Cultures!

How do you keep a humble attitude while learning a new language and culture? How do you respond when people laugh at you when you are learning a foreign language?

Chapter Ten

The Powerful Importance of Prepositions

While learning Arabic in Morocco, we would often have people laugh when we made mistakes in our pronunciation or vocabulary choice.

I would always ask, "Are you laughing WITH me or are you laughing AT me?!"

That small preposition makes a big difference! "WITH" or "AT" changes the entire meaning of the sentence.

Our Moroccan friends would typically say, "Of course we are not laughing AT you! We are laughing WITH you!"

In response, I would say, "I'm so glad that my language learning and language mistakes make you happy. If that's the only reason I'm here in your country—to spread a little joy—it's all worth it!"

Tiny, Yet Powerful

Prepositions make an enormous difference in meaning.

It reminds me of a recent conversation with my husband, Vincent, at the gym. We were doing our regular work out together, side-by-side on the elliptical machines. We were sweating—with hearts pumping hard—trying to burn calories and eliminate toxins from our bodies. As usual, Vincent was jamming to music, and I was listening to one of my favorite podcasts.

Suddenly, I noticed Vincent took out his earplugs.

I took out mine as well and asked, "What's wrong?"

"My phone just pooped on me," he said.

I laughed out loud, and Vincent didn't know why.

"Your phone pooped OUT on you. It didn't 'poop ON you,'" I explained.

Vincent realized at that point what he had said and smiled.

"A bird can 'poop on you,' but a phone dies, runs out of battery, and 'poops OUT on you,'" I told him, the language teacher resurrecting inside of me.

It's amazing what a difference a tiny word, a small preposition, can make in the meaning of a sentence.

Let's Weave Cultures!

Think about prepositions like "on, under, out, with, to . . ." What other sentences do you know that change meaning entirely when you add, remove, or change a preposition? Small words can have a lot of importance and meaning. Beware!

Chapter Eleven

What is the Cost of a Language Barrier?

*"I love commuting between languages just like I
love commuting between cultures and cities."* –
Elif Safak

On our first day in Spain, we went to the town hall to begin our residential paperwork. We followed our other expat friends who had already been on the ground for several years and who spoke Spanish fluently.

There were a few tiny spaces near the town hall, but we didn't want to try to squeeze in. Rather, we followed our friends to an area further away with a lot of wide, open spaces. No "squeezing in" required!

Long Enough!

We were only in the town hall for twenty minutes—just long enough!

When we got to our vehicles, we all noticed parking tickets on our windshields. Ugh oh!

Forty euros!

Our eyes were suddenly opened. We looked up and noticed that we were parked directly in front of the entrance of the local police station. A clearly marked sign in Spanish hung just above our cars. It said, "Official vehicles only." The curb was also painted bright sunshine yellow.

"Warning! Don't park here!" it screamed.

"Sorry!"

My husband, Vincent, and I walked up to a police officer standing nearby and spoke in English. "Hola, we are so sorry. We don't speak Spanish. Our family just arrived in Spain yesterday. We are sorry that we didn't know."

He pointed to the "no parking" sign and then pointed to the counter where we could pay for the parking ticket.

No grace for us today!

Language barriers can surely be costly.

"That was such a great cultural learning experience," Vincent said, as he walked back to our car after paying the parking ticket.

"I'm glad you had fun. Let's try to find some free language and cultural learning lessons from here on out," I replied with a grin.

Let's Weave Cultures!

Have you ever traveled to a foreign country and had to pay the price for a language barrier? What happened?

Chapter Twelve
Mistakes With False Cognates

D o you remember hearing the word "cognate" when learning a foreign language in high school or college?

Cambridge Dictionary describes a cognate as "a word that has the same origin as another word, or is related to another word."

Cognates usually look alike and have the same meaning.

For example, the Italian word *"mangiare"* (= to eat) is cognate with the French word *"manger"* (=to eat). These two words are cognates. Other examples are "problem" in English and *"problema"* in Spanish or "helicopter" in English and *"hélicoptère"* in French.

Cognates in Learning Spanish

At the time, our family had been living in Spain for four months, and all of us were learning Spanish. Thankfully, because French and Spanish are both Latin languages, there are a lot of cognates between the two languages.

Since we already knew French, we could see and recognize cognates in Spanish and understand a lot more than someone who didn't know French or another Latin-based language.

The high school Spanish teacher, for example, told us that our son, David, was learning Spanish quickly—and even had the highest grade in the class. (I was a proud mama!) This may have seemed surprising, since all the other students had been living in Spain for years. However, David could "cheat" with all the cognates between French and Spanish.

That all sounds great, huh, for learning a foreign language?

Beware of False Cognates!

However, we must beware of "false cognates"! Not all words mean the same thing—especially when you are an English speaker learning French!

False cognates are words that look identical in two languages, but their meanings are different. They are like twins—they look identical, but they are very different inside!

In French, we call them "*faux amis*," literally translated as "false friends."

Believe me, they are not always friendly! These "*faux amis*" can get you into a lot of trouble.

"These words can easily trick you into getting the wrong end of the stick, or to saying something senseless or embarrassing that you hadn't intended at all." {1}

Fluent U lists "20 Common French False Friends to Watch Out For":

—*Ancien*/Ancient (former / ancient, old)

—*Attendre*/Attend (to wait / to attend)

—*Bras*/Bras (arm / bras)

—*Brasserie*/Brassiere (brewery, pub / bra)

—*Blessé*/Blessed (wounded, injured / blessed)

—*Bouton*/Button (pimple / button)

—*Monnaie*/Money (coins, change / money (coins and bills))

—*Déception*/Deception (disappointment / deception)

—*Envie*/Envy (desire / envy)

—*Grand*/Grand (big / great)

—*Grappe*/Grape (bunch / grape)

—*Joli*/Jolly (pretty / jolly)

—*Journée*/Journey (day / journey)

—*Librairie*/Library (bookstore / library)

—*Location*/Location (rental / location)

—*Coin*/Coin (corner / coin)

—*Passer*/Pass (to take—ex. a test / to pass)

—*Prune*/Prune (plum / prune)

—*Raisin*/Raisin (grape / raisin)

—*Préservatif*/Preservative (condom / preservative)

Boy! I sure wish that I would have had this list in my high school French class. It could have spared me from the BIG, EMBARRASSING BLOOPER I made when I had lunch with my French family a few years later.

I will never forget that *préservatif* and preservative are FALSE COGNATES . . . and FALSE FRIENDS!

Whatever foreign language you are learning, make sure you study the false cognates. Unless, like me, you don't mind making lots of hilarious—and embarrassing—language bloopers!

LET'S WEAVE CULTURES!

Do you know any *"faux amis"* in other languages? When and where did you accidentally use them? How did you know you had made a mistake? What did you do when you realized?

{1} Fluent U: https://www.fluentu.com/blog/french/faux-amis-french-false-friends-cognates/

Chapter Thirteen

The Danger of Learning a Language Orally

"Language is wine upon the lips."
– Virginia Woolf

Language learning is dangerous . . . truly dangerous!

As I wrote in my story, "I Learned My Spanish in Zumba Class," sometimes we learn foreign words and expressions out of context. This can lead to some misunderstanding, confusion, and downright embarrassment!

This happened when I was studying in France as a young adult, learning French with my husband, Vincent, and his "buddies" in the village. I did not know what level of language I was learning (slang, informal, formal, etc.). All I knew was what the word meant—or so I thought—and then I used it and repeated it.

Oops! That can lead to a lot of language bloopers.

You may remember the story of my future, French mother-in-law and how I used the word "drunk" out of context. I had learned a vulgar slang word, and I didn't even know it. When I repeated it to an older woman who deserved my utmost respect . . . well, it was offensive! Oops!

Treading on Dangerous Terrain!

As we are now walking down the fun and challenging road of language learning once again—this time in Spain—we are treading on some dangerous terrain.

We are using an oral language learning method called Growing Participator Approach (GPA). It is a learner-led approach, so Vincent and I plan the lessons ahead of time to work on with our language helper. We have several Spanish tutors in order to be exposed to a variety of expressions, vocabulary, and accents.

One day, we went for our language lesson at our tutor's nail salon. It was great to learn language in a natural working context where she was having live and real interactions with customers.

Learning Orally With Wordless Picture Books

That day, we were learning greetings and how to say "hello" to someone in the morning, afternoon, and evening. We were using "wordless" picture books, so the language tutor was free to input her own dialogue—whatever was most natural for her.

The picture we were looking at showed two women meeting on the street.

"*Hola, Guapa!*" our language helper said as she pointed to the dialogue "bubbles" over the heads of the illustrated women.

In Spanish (Our language tutor didn't speak English.), we attempted to understand the context of this new word, "*guapa.*" Our tutor told us that it can be used to greet a woman. She said that Vincent could say it to me, for example, or I could say it to another female friend.

At that moment, a regular client walked through the door.

"*Hola, Guapa!*" our tutor said, demonstrating the use of this word in a natural context.

"*Hola!*" the woman replied with a smile.

It seemed simple enough, so we moved on to the next dialogue of greetings and completed our lesson.

Practice Makes Perfect!

On the way home from the nail salon, we stopped at a local bakery to pick up a loaf of bread for lunch. It was a bakery that we went to from time to time. A young man was behind the counter. I asked where his mother was. She was an older, friendly woman who was usually there. The young man explained that the woman wasn't his mother, but his aunt. The kind woman came out from the backroom and greeted us.

Vincent was eager to use his new vocabulary words. It is highly recommended to use new words and expressions as soon as you learn them in order to cement them into your brain.

"*Hola, Guapa!*" he said.

We noticed a look of surprise on the faces of the woman and her nephew. We asked how she was doing, as well as her family. Vincent then chose our favorite type of bread (warm in the wrapped paper), paid, and said goodbye.

How Could We Have Known?

Several weeks later, our son, David, asked me if I could quiz him for his Spanish test the next day. He handed me his textbook, opened to the list of vocabulary words and expressions that he needed to learn.

The title of the word list said, "Appearance."

"Oh, this might be good for me to learn," I thought to myself.

My eyes quickly scanned the list of words, and the word "*guapo (a)*" jumped out at me from the page.

It said, "*guapo (a) — good-looking.*"

"Oh, my goodness!" I screeched, and then began laughing hysterically. David didn't know why, so I explained to him what had happened at the bakery a few weeks before.

I put on my cultural awareness glasses and did some research. Here's what I found.

"When I first arrived in Spain, I had several men say to me 'Guapa.' I had no idea what it meant as it's an adjective only used in Spanish in Spain, so I had to look it up on the Internet.

I soon found out Guapa, (or Guapo, if the word is said to a man), means 'Beautiful' or 'Handsome' in English. But most Spaniards will tell you, it's often used not just to mean beautiful or handsome, but also to mean a kind of beauty or handsomeness that is also very sexy.

Guapa or Guapo are also often used as something to call someone — for instance:

"Hola guapa. ¿Cómo estás?" — Hey, Beautiful. How are you?" [2]

How Embarrassing!

When Vincent came home that evening, I told him that when he went into the bakery the other day, he said to the older woman, "Hey, Good Looking!"

I showed him David's Spanish textbook, and he shook his head in disbelief.

Although we love *"Guapa's"* fresh bread, I think we will be choosing another bakery from now on!

LET'S WEAVE CULTURES!

What language bloopers have you made in learning a foreign language? Did you learn and use words or expressions "out of context," not fully understanding the meaning?

[2]https://seriouslyspain.com/what-does-the-spanish-word-guapaguapo-mean-in-english

Chapter Fourteen

A Mistress?!

We wandered the mall, enjoying time with our good friends from Canada. It was the big time of sales, *"rebajas"* in Spanish, held only a few times a year. Our oldest son, Timothée, was looking for some clothes. He found a jacket that he liked, so we scrambled through the racks looking for his size—medium. There was none to be found. We found a size large and wondered if it could fit him. He tried it on, too big.

Our friend had a sewing machine and was skilled in designing and making clothes, backpacks, and purses.

"It would be easy to take it in," his wife said, as she studied the jacket on our son.

"Oh, right!" my French husband said, "You have your own personal mistress!"

We all laughed out loud, and my husband looked puzzled.

"Seamstress, not mistress!" I said. "And for a man, we say 'tailor.'"

LET'S WEAVE CULTURES!

What language bloopers have you made in learning a foreign language?

Chapter Fifteen
"Who's Jorge?"

*"A special kind of beauty exists which is born in
language, of language, and for language."* –
Gaston Bachelard

"**R**ead, *Jorge*," Those were the only two words that I heard in my broken Spanish. "*Jorge*" is pronounced "Hor-hey" in Spanish.

I turned to my husband, Vincent, and said, "What book of the Bible is that —*Jorge*?"

At that time, a man was walking towards the front of the church.

"It's not a book of the Bible. It's the name of the man who was called up to read the passage."

"Right," I whispered into my husband's ear, laughing out loud. "There is no *Book of George* in the Bible, is there?"

LET'S WEAVE CULTURES!

What language bloopers have you made in learning a foreign language?

Part 3

Funny Food

Chapter Sixteen
Can I Make it a 'Coke Float' Please?

S panish language learning can be challenging and fun—or should I say FUNNY!?

Driving four hours from Barcelona to Madrid, we made a pit stop in Zaragoza. It was about half-way on our journey, and we all needed some time to stretch our legs, go to the potty, and grab something cold to drink for the road.

What we thought would be a quick pit stop turned into an amazing cultural and linguistic experience!

After visiting the town for thirty minutes, we found a small tapas bar where we could go to the restroom for free, and get something to drink.

The Strange Order

My husband, Vincent, and I ordered Cokes, and our son, Pierre, chose his favorite orange Fanta.

The lady placed our cold cans of soda on the bar counter. She asked us if we wanted plastic glasses to take with us.

"*No, Gracias,*" Vincent said in Spanish. ("No, thank you.")

"*Si, si,*" I replied. "*Basso con helado.*" ("Yes, yes, a cup with ice cream.")

The lady looked at me strangely, and I wasn't sure why.

"*Helado?*" she asked.

When I heard her say it out loud, I immediately recognized my language error.

Funny Spanish Language Learning—That's Not What I Meant!

"*No helado,*" I replied. "*Hielo.*" ("No ice cream, ice.")

We all laughed together. I quickly grabbed my plastic cup with ice cubes and my can of Coke, and walked as fast as I could out of the tapas bar.

Why Not??

As I stepped outside, I thought about my language mistake and my request for ice cream instead of ice in my cup. Actually, it wasn't such a crazy request. I come from the land of "root beer floats"! For those who don't know this sweet American treat, it consists of vanilla ice cream and root beer soda. Why couldn't I have a "Coke float"—vanilla ice cream with Coke?

Curiously, I looked it up. Although I've never had a Coke float, people drink them all the time. You can make an ice cream float with any type of ice cream and soda you want. And, what I thought to be an American dessert is actually known in many countries around the world!

Here's what I discovered when I put on my cultural awareness lenses and became a "cultural learner."

Did You Know?

"An ice cream float or ice cream soda (United States, United Kingdom, Canada, South Africa and East Asia), coke float (United States, United Kingdom, and Southeast Asia), or spider (Australia and New Zealand), is a chilled beverage that consists of ice cream in either a soft drink or in a mixture of flavored syrup and carbonated water. When root beer and ice cream are used together to make the beverage, it is typically referred to as a root beer float (United States and Canada)." —**Wikipedia**

Maybe I'll run back inside the tapas bar and introduce this American speciality to the Spanish world!

In the meantime, I better keep working on my Spanish language learning. After learning Spanish in Zumba class, I obviously have a long way to go!

LET'S WEAVE CULTURES!

What funny language mistakes and bloopers have you made when learning a foreign language? How did you handle it?

Chapter Seventeen

Funny Stomach Pain

*"Speak a new language so that the world will be
a new world."* – Rumi

My husband, Vincent, bought his cherries at the local outdoor market, and he enjoyed eating his cherries all day long. Until . . .

We went on an evening stroll, *paseo*, in the neighborhood with our friends who had come over for dinner that night. We didn't get very far before Vincent tapped me on the shoulder and told me he would have to return to the house. He had stomach cramps and was in extreme pain. Too many cherries.

"How many did you eat?" I asked.

"Too many," he replied.

Too Many!

When I went home, I looked at the wooden crate of cherries that we had purchased that morning at the outdoor market down the street—two kilos' worth. It was over half-empty, which meant that Vincent had consumed over one kilo of cherries in the past ten hours. No wonder he was doubled over with pain.

The next morning, he was relaying the story to our sons, Timothée and Robert.

"I was in so much pain. It felt like my stomach was going to rapture!" Vincent exclaimed.

Timothée started chuckling quietly, and then we all looked at each other with amusement.

Vincent repeated the same word, "rapture," multiple times in the telling of his story, which made it even funnier for the rest of us.

Timothée pronounced the two words distinctly so his father could hear the difference.

"RAPTURE and RUPTURE," he enunciated.

Vincent finally caught on and said, "Actually, it's true, I thought my stomach might rupture from the cherries, and that I might die and be raptured into heaven! My stomach would have to go with me!"

We started laughing so hard that we all thought our stomachs would "rapture"!

Let's Weave Cultures!

Have you ever made a language mistake and blooper, because you swapped one little letter—like rUpture and rApture?

Chapter Eighteen
The Language Barrier at the Drive-Thru

"Do you know what a foreign accent is? A sign of bravery." —Amy Chua

We were living in the United States at the time. It was Friday night—our family's "Pizza Night." Usually, it was Pizza Hut, or better yet, Papa Vincent's homemade pizza. That night, we all wanted something besides pizza, and no one wanted to cook.

Along with our kids, we finally decided on one of the all-time American fast-food favorites, "KFC"—"Kentucky Fried Chicken." My husband, Vincent, and I went through the drive-thru.

I love drive-thrus. There's no reason to get out of the car. We were too tired and too lazy for that. If you are going to eat fast food, make it easy.

The Black Box

Vincent was behind the wheel that night, which meant that he would be the one with the honors of placing our food order with the "invisible person behind the black box." Seems simple enough . . . unless you are in a small American town in rural Pennsylvania and you have a French accent.

"Hello, may I take your order?" the lady's voice boomed through the drive-thru speaker.

"We will take a 12-piece chicken tender bucket," Vincent said.

"Could you repeat that, please?" she asked.

I understood Vincent perfectly, so why couldn't the invisible woman behind the black box?

After several attempts at ordering the "12-piece chicken tender bucket, potato wedges, and macaroni and cheese," the American fast-food employee gave up.

What?!

"Sir, could you please drive forward to the window to place your order?"

"What?! Can she not understand me?!" Vincent exclaimed with frustration.

"I can understand you just fine," I replied, trying to reassure my husband. "These people just aren't used to foreign accents. There's a language barrier."

Through a mixture of laughter and impatience, Vincent yelled out the window, "I want to go somewhere where people can understand my accent!"

Upon arriving at the drive-thru window, the woman apologized for not being able to understand Vincent through the speaker. In turn, he apologized for his French accent. "Pardon my French!"

Did he really need to apologize for his foreign accent?

Bi-Lingual Devices?

Exiting the parking lot, Vincent and I laughed together about the incident. We reassured each other that we would soon leave mono-cultural, mono-lingual rural Pennsylvania and head back to the international world of Europe. In Europe, there are so many accents represented, you just get used to them!

The same "language barrier at the drive-thru" phenomenon takes place when Vincent tries to communicate with Amazon's "Alexa" device, Xfinity's nifty "voice control" function on the TV remote control, or the famous "Siri" on Apple devices.

The other day, Vincent pushed the voice control button on our remote and asked for "The World of Dancing," one of our son's favorite shows. I cannot recall what appeared on the TV screen, but it was NOT "The World of Dancing." Vincent tried multiple times and then called me over for help. He needed my American accent.

These mono-lingual devices do not understand foreign accents! There is a language barrier.

Let's Weave Cultures!

How do you respond when someone speaks to you with a foreign accent? If you have learned a foreign language, have you ever had someone react to your accent? What did you do to cross that language barrier?

Chapter Nineteen

The Surprise in My Milkshake!

"You have to taste a culture to understand it." —

Deborah Cater

"My milkshake tasted weird," our son, David, told us as we pulled out of the Dairy Queen parking lot.

We had just enjoyed a nice evening with some friends from church. There were not a ton of things to do in our small rural town, but going to Dairy Queen was one of our favorites.

"What was wrong with it?" I asked David. "What kind of milkshake did you order?"

"A chocolate *frappé*," he replied. "I saw it on the menu."

I smiled and chuckled quietly to myself.

French Memories

Memories flooded my mind as I recalled the many after-school trips to McDonald's with our boys in France. On hard days, on days of celebration, or on "normal" days just to connect with my kids, we would often go through the McDonalds' drive-thru next to their school for an ice cream treat.

Unfortunately, in France, there were very few ice cream treats at McDonalds —sundaes and *frappés*. *Frappés* were as close as you could get to an American milkshake, yet still so far away. David always ordered chocolate *frappés*. Those were his favorite. That night in America, he had wanted a chocolate *frappé*, but that is clearly not what he got!

Not the Same Thing!

In the U.S., a *frappé* is NOT a milkshake.

According to Wikipedia, "Frappé coffee (also Greek frappé or café frappé) is a Greek iced coffee drink made from instant coffee (generally, *Nescafé*), water and sugar. Accidentally invented by a *Nescafé* representative named Dimitris Vakondios in 1957 in the city of Thessaloniki, frappé is sold primarily in Greece and is among the most popular drinks in Greece and Cyprus, and is available at virtually all Greek cafés. The word *frappé* comes from the French word *frapper*, meaning 'to hit', as crushed ice does when mixed with a drink and shaken in a cocktail shaker. The frappé has become a hallmark of post-war outdoor Greek coffee culture."

"In America, a *frappé* is an iced coffee drink," I explained to David. "I guess you just drank your first iced coffee with chocolate flavoring. You may have a hard time sleeping tonight with all that caffeine."

"Oh, that's why it tasted so weird!" he replied.

"Why didn't you tell us or tell the Dairy Queen employee that it tasted weird?"

"I just thought that was what American chocolate milkshakes tasted like!" he said.

FYI: An American "milkshake is a sweet, cold beverage that is usually made from milk, ice cream, or iced milk, and flavorings or sweeteners such as butterscotch, caramel sauce, chocolate syrup, or fruit syrup." Wikipedia

Let's Weave Cultures!

Have you ever ordered something in a foreign country and got something completely different from what you had imagined or expected?

Chapter Twenty

What Kind of Water Do You Drink?

During a recent trip to Germany, my husband, Vincent, went to the local supermarket to get some groceries. He came back with a six-pack of bottled water. I'm not sure why he got the water. German water is just fine to drink.

He opened up the first bottle and heard "psst." He realized he had purchased "gassy" carbonated water. Vincent likes carbonated water. I don't. Neither do our kids.

'Classic' Doesn't Mean 'Normal'

"It said 'classic,' on the bottle, so I thought that meant 'normal,'" Vincent stated. Obviously not. The next day, we returned to the supermarket to get "normal" water or "still" water. There it was, written in bold on the plastic bottle—"still." When I saw that word, it reminded me of a story that a friend recently told me about his first traveling adventure in Europe.

'Still' or 'Active'?

In a restaurant, the server asked him if he wanted "still" or "active" water.

He did not know what that meant, but laughed and responded, "I don't know. It would be nice to have my water sitting long enough in a glass for me to drink it. Perhaps 'still' water would be best. I certainly don't want 'active' water that will jump out of the glass!"

If you haven't traveled the world, you may have never heard the expressions "still" and "active" water. "Still" water is "normal" or "regular" water, sometimes called "flat" water, and "active" water is "carbonated" or "sparkling" water with active gas bubbles. There are all kinds of different words for "still" water. On a recent flight with a Spanish airline, the flight attendant asked me if I wanted "natural" water. I wasn't sure what she meant until she said, "Natural or gassy water?"

"Natural water," I replied with a smile.

Carbonated water is water that has been infused with carbon dioxide gas under pressure. This produces a bubbly drink that's also known as sparkling water, club soda, soda water, seltzer water and fizzy water. Except for seltzer water, carbonated waters usually have salt added to improve the taste. Sometimes small amounts of other minerals are included. —Healthline

If you travel in Europe and in many parts of the world, be prepared for this question whenever you order water. Do you want your water sitting "still" in your glass or do you want it "actively" swimming around?

Let's Weave Cultures!

When you have traveled the world, have you had some funny or interesting experiences when ordering food and drinks?

https://www.healthline.com/nutrition/carbonated-water-good-or-bad

Chapter Twenty-One

Why Do You Have to Say 'Bon Appetit'?

"Any time you think some other language is strange, remember that yours is just as strange, you're just used to it." – Anonymous

We recently had dinner with some American friends who arrived in France two years before. We were laughing together in the kitchen, as they recounted one of their recent cultural bloopers.

They had invited a French family over for a meal. Everyone had been served. They had prayed a blessing for the meal, but no one was eating. They couldn't figure out why.

After some awkward silence and uncomfortable space, our friends realized that they had failed to say *"Bon appétit!"* to their guests.

These two small words—meaning "Enjoy your meal!"—give the signal that one can begin eating.

Thankfully, they realized this sooner than later . . . or that French family might still be sitting at their dining room table just waiting to dive into the food!

"Bon appétit!"—a phrase, originally from French, meaning "good appetite," said to someone who is about to eat, meaning, "I hope you enjoy your food." —Cambridge Dictionary

It made me think of our days in Morocco. Before a meal with our local friends, one would say, *"Bismillah"* which means, "In the name of God." This sacred word and blessing would be proclaimed whenever there was a new "undertaking" or something "beginning"—like eating a meal, entering a house for the first time, driving a new car, etc.

Before a meal, it was a prayer to thank God for the meal placed before them. Once these words were spoken, everyone could eat—but not a moment before.

Let's Weave Cultures!

What about you—in your own culture or in places where you have traveled? Are there words or blessings that must be spoken before one can eat?

Chapter Twenty-Two

Tapas Are Included in the Price

O ne of our first nights in our new house in Spain—just after our late-evening dinner—we went out for an evening stroll to the tapas bar just down the street.

It was still hot in Spain, and the evening air and cold drinks would hopefully cool us off. Each of us ordered a beverage.

The server took our order and then pointed to the pictures of *tapas* on the menu. She was clearly asking us what *tapas* we wanted.

A tapa is an appetizer or snack in Spanish cuisine. It may be cold (such as mixed olives and cheese) or hot (such as *chopitos*, which are battered, fried, baby squid). In some bars and restaurants in Spain and across the globe, tapas have evolved into a more sophisticated cuisine. Tapas can be combined to make a full meal. —Wikipedia

Having just finished dinner an hour earlier, we weren't hungry.

"No Tapas!"

"No tapas," I said with an American accent.

The server looked surprised and said, *"No? Niño?"* ("No? The boy?") She was especially shocked that we weren't ordering food for our youngest child, Pierre.

I wanted to explain to her we had just finished dinner and weren't hungry, but the language barrier between us prohibited me.

"*No tapas*," I repeated.

"Ok," she responded with a shrug of her shoulders.

She walked away, perplexed.

"They are Free!"

"You know the tapas are free with your drinks?" Timothée asked me.

"What? Are you kidding? I didn't know that," I exclaimed.

Vincent explained to me he had recently gone to a *tapas* bar at the airport with Timothée. They each ordered a drink, and they got TWO FREE *tapas* with each beverage. Wow!

I quickly grabbed my phone and went straight to the "Google Translate" app. Plugging in the sentence, "Are *tapas* free with our beverages?" I looked at the Spanish translation.

As soon as I could call her back over, I showed the server my phone and my question in Spanish.

"*Sí!*" she responded with a smile.

"No Comprendo!"

"Oh," I said, "*No Comprendo.*"

I was an ignorant tourist who couldn't speak the language.

She counted the beverages on our table. "*Uno, dos, tres, cuatro, cinco, seis.*" Then, she pointed to the pictures of the *tapas* on the menu and counted again, "*Uno, dos, tres, cuatro, cinco, seis.*"

We selected six different *tapas* for a variety—chicken nuggets for Pierre, cheeseburgers for Timothée and David, a grilled cheese sandwich for Robert, fried calamari for Vincent, and French fries for me. We ate all of it, even though we had just left the dinner table at our house one hour earlier. We didn't want to pass up the freebies!

Our final receipt indeed showed 0,00 euros for each tapa. They were completely free and included with the purchase of the drinks.

A Cheap and Easy Meal

"Wow!" I said to Vincent. "We should come here for dinner every night. For 3,10 euros, we can order a Coke and get a free cheeseburger, chicken nuggets, calamari sandwich . . . We could try a different tapa for dinner every night, and that would make a cheap and easy meal!"

FYI, a *tapa* (sometimes 2!) is almost always included with your drink, so don't miss out! I guess I should read "Culture Shock: Spain" or "Spain: Culture Smart." Then, I would know these cultural tidbits! I clearly lacked cultural awareness. It was time for me to become a "cultural learner."

When we think of "culture shock," we usually think of something negative. I have to say that this "culture shock" tidbit is VERY positive and a highlight of the Spanish culture.

Siestas and free *tapas* . . . thank you, God, for bringing our family to Spain. I think I'm going to like it here!

Let's Weave Cultures!

Have you ever missed out on something because you lacked cultural awareness when traveling or living in a foreign country? What did you do to become a cultural learner?

Chapter Twenty-Three
What in the World is "Fuzzy Water"?

*"It is astonishing how much enjoyment one can
get out of a language that one understands
imperfectly."*
–Basil Gildersleeve

"I provide a lot of content for your blog," my husband, Vincent, said to me one day while driving into the city. "Good thing I make a lot of language bloopers."

Yes, good thing!

Here we go again—another funny conversation over a meal.

More Options to Choose From

You may remember the story, "What Kind of Water Do You Drink?" In restaurants in Europe, it's very common to be asked this question. The options in Spain are *"aqua sin gaz"* or *"aqua con gaz"* (still water or sparkling water).

At our house, sparkling water is often called "fizzy water."

Recently, my husband asked our son, David, to pass the bottle of sparkling water to him at the dinner table.

"Can you please pass me the fuzzy water?" he asked.

We all started laughing. As usual, it took Vincent a few seconds to realize what in the world he had just said. What could make us smile at each other and chuckle out loud?

What Do You Mean?

He meant to say "fizzy" water, but it didn't quite come out that way.

So, I now have to add this "new" type of water to the list of options in my story, "What Kind of Water Do You Drink?"

Beware! If you order sparkling water at our house, you may find little "fuzzies" floating around in your glass.

Perhaps from our dog's fur, a nearby dandelion, fuzzies from a favorite soft sweater . . .

Let's Weave Cultures!

Have you ever accidentally changed one little letter or one little sound in a word—transforming your normal sentence into one that made you chuckle?

Chapter Twenty-Four
Eggs Vs. Apples

Three days a week, I had been going to the local community center for my Spanish classes. Sometimes I dreaded going, and it was a struggle to get out the door and to class on time. However, once I was there, I loved it.

I love languages—the challenge, the mystery, the humor. I also love being among people just like me—foreigners, immigrants, strangers in another land. We are all struggling together—struggling to learn a new language, struggling to adjust to a foreign culture, struggling to settle in a country far from family and friends.

Our recent chapter was on food. It was fun to learn about the Spanish culture through its food and local dishes. *Paella, tortilla, churros, calamares, tapas . . .*

The teacher was talking to us about eggs and different ways to cook them. I asked her how to write "scrambled eggs." As she wrote the words on the chalkboard, she asked us what we needed to make eggs. Several of us shouted out different vocabulary words that we had recently learned —"eggs" and "oil" seemed to be the most common ingredients.

Better to Keep My Mouth Shut!

Wanting to practice my Spanish-speaking skills, I continued. "In the United States, in my family, when we make scrambled eggs, we add a little bit of milk," I said proudly.

The teacher looked at me, surprised. "Milk?" she asked.

"Yes," I said. "*Y, en mi familia, no utilisamos aciete, pero manzana.*" (Translation: "And, in my family, we don't use oil to make scrambled eggs, but apples.")

"*Manzana?*" the teacher said, with a bewildered look on her face.

"*Si, manzana,*" I continued. "In the United States, we don't use as much oil for cooking as you do here in Spain. We prefer apples to cook our eggs."

I noticed that everyone in my class seemed surprised and confused. However, that didn't shock me too much. Most of my fellow Spanish students were Moroccan and Nigerian. In their cultures, the more oil, the better! The teacher seemed even more shocked at my persistent chatter, but finally moved on to another topic. Enough about eggs and apples!

Confusion Realization!

That evening, at home, my husband took the butter out of the refrigerator. As a highly motivated Spanish learner, he is always speaking Spanish—practicing his new vocabulary and pronunciation.

"*Mantequilla,*" he said as he placed the butter on the counter.

"*Mantequilla!*" I screamed. "Not *manzana!*"

My husband looked at me, confused.

"I told my teacher and my class that we cook scrambled eggs in America with apples, not oil!"

"What?" he said. "Did you confuse *manzana* (apple) and *mantequilla* (butter)?"

"I sure did!" I said, laughing.

Laughing at Myself

The next day, I went to class and explained to everyone that I had realized my mistake. They all laughed.

"It seemed surprising," my teacher said. "However, I know Americans like to eat peanut butter with apples, so I thought that perhaps they also like to eat their eggs with apples!"

Everyone laughed, and I laughed right along with them!

We have to always remember that, yes, learning a language requires a lot of blood, sweat, and tears. However, we cannot leave out a good dose of laughter in the process! I'm convinced that our few moments of chuckling together over my language blooper put us all in a more relaxed state, making our brains better prepared to absorb another hour of Spanish language!

Let's Weave Cultures!

Have you ever learned a foreign language? What has been your funniest language blooper? How did you handle it when people laughed at your mistake?

Part 4

Cultural Mishaps

Chapter Twenty-Five

A Lesson—Don't Stir Middle Eastern Coffee!

"Those who know nothing of foreign languages
know nothing of their own.
— Johann Wolfgang von Goethe

My first visit to a Syrian home in France was full of cultural learning and cultural mistakes!

Rabia, my new Syrian refugee friend, proudly brought out her coffee (قهوة, in Arabic, pronounced *"qa-hu-a"*), served in fine porcelain—all donated items. She poured the thick, black syrup into the small, *demitasse* coffee cups.

She was happy to welcome me into her home, demonstrating her priceless cultural gift of hospitality.

The smell of the coffee was strong, made with *cardamom*, a spice with a strong, resinous aroma and a sweet flavor. *Cardamom* is a key ingredient of Syrian and Turkish coffee.

I wasn't a coffee drinker. I was a tea drinker, and I especially loved North African mint tea. This Middle Eastern culture was very different and new to me. I had a lot to learn.

As usual, I wanted to respect and honor my hostess and her gift. Coffee in Middle Eastern culture was of utmost importance. Refusing to accept and drink her fine coffee could have been offensive to her, leading to a barrier in our relationship . . . rather than a bridge. I wanted to integrate and not offend. I accepted.

No Sugar, No Spoon

Thankfully, the cup of coffee was small. Hopefully, I could get it down.

I took a sip of the hot, bitter beverage and grimaced. Rabia chuckled when I asked her for more sugar. She told me that one rarely adds sugar after the coffee has been made. Any sugar or milk would need to be added before boiling. The *cardamom* seed was already naturally sweet.

I added the sugar cube and then realized that I needed to stir my coffee. I asked Rabia for a spoon and stirred the dark liquid inside my cup. That really made her giggle, as she told me that one must not stir Syrian coffee. I didn't understand why I shouldn't stir my coffee, but I laughed right along with her.

"Sediment" Coffee

I sipped it slowly, praying all the way! I quickly learned why I shouldn't have stirred the coffee. It had stirred up everything that was supposed to stay at the bottom of the cup! Every sip left strong bits of coffee grounds in my mouth—not a good taste. I learned quickly that Syrian coffee, like traditional *Türk kahvesi* (Turkish coffee), is not processed through a filter. Rather, it is a "sediment coffee," boiled in a tiny coffee pan.

Don't drink immediately after the Turkish coffee has been served. Give the sediment time to settle down in its tiny cup before you take your first sip. **—Marc Guillet: "How to Drink Turkish Coffee" (Enjoy-Istambul.com)**

When I slowly arrived at the mound of coffee grounds at the bottom of the cup, I quickly realized that I would be wise to not drink those. I laughed at myself again.

Thankfully, according to their tradition, Rabia had served me a glass of cold tap water alongside my coffee. I would soon learn that the glass of water was not meant to wash away the coffee sediment that had accidentally made its way into my mouth. Rather, it should refresh and awaken my taste buds . . . leading to a much more enjoyable coffee-drinking experience.

A Memorable Visit—Much More Than Coffee

confess, I drank the water that day to wash those unwelcomed grounds out of my mouth. My first coffee experience with my new Syrian friend had been far from enjoyable for my taste buds.

My first home visit with my new Syrian friend, however, was one of the most enriching cultural experiences in my book of life. It is also one that we will both always remember, as it sparked a lot of healthy laughter in our budding friendship.

Upon leaving Rabia's home a few hours later, I noticed a strong "buzz" feeling as I walked to the metro station. As the train began moving and swaying along the tracks, I felt as if I were drunk! That Syrian coffee was extremely strong, especially for this novice coffee drinker.

I have learned throughout the years that it is best for me to politely decline coffee in the homes of my Syrian friends. When I tell them I don't drink coffee, they are surprised. However, when I tell them I love tea, they smile graciously and then turn on the hot water . . . eager to prepare me a glass of Syrian tea (شاي in Arabic, pronounced *"shay"*).

How to Make Middle Eastern Coffee:

10 Minutes

Ingredients:

1 cup water

1 tablespoon finely ground Arabic coffee (cocoa powder consistency)

1/8 ground teaspoon *cardamom* (1 seed pod)

Optional: sugar and/or milk

(Makes 2 servings)

Directions:

Grind some *cardamom* seeds with a pestle (a tool with a rounded end), and crush them very finely. Boil water in a *cezve* or *ibrik* (traditional Turkish coffee pot), or a regular saucepan, then, remove from heat. Add finely ground coffee (cocoa powder consistency) and the crushed *cardamom* (and optional sugar and/or milk). Heat and simmer the coffee until it begins to boil and foam forms on the top. Serve your hot coffee in small, tall glasses. Remember to allow the coffee to rest for a few minutes before serving, so that the grounds can settle on the bottom of the cup. Serve with a glass of cold water. Above all, DO NOT STIR! Enjoy!

— **Recipe adapted from "The Spruce Eats" (www.thespruceeats.com)**

Let's Weave Cultures!

Try this Middle Eastern coffee recipe, even if you can't find cardamom, or share other variations of coffee recipes from your part of the world. Tell us about your experience.

Have you ever made a cultural mistake when eating or drinking in the home of someone from another country or culture? If so, how did you react? How did the other person react? What did you learn from this "*faux-pas*"?

Chapter Twenty-Six

Why Do You Close the Bathroom Door?

While sharing a meal with some global friends recently, we discussed the intriguing topic of toilets and bathrooms—and cultural differences. It's quite a stimulating cultural topic, and I highly recommend that you join in the conversation.

Unnecessary Waiting

Many times, in my very own home, I have waited impatiently in front of a closed door for very long minutes—waiting for someone to come out of the bathroom. I have pictured a person sitting on the "throne" with a magazine or cell phone, lingering for way too long. I ask myself, "What in the world are they doing in there for so long?!"

After waiting for what seems like an eternity, I'm often shocked to discover that the "someone" was actually "no one." There was no one in the bathroom! Then why in the world was the bathroom door closed?!?!

Why IN THE WORLD was the door closed?! And WHERE IN THE WORLD do people close bathroom doors when there is NO ONE in the bathroom?!?! The answer to this question is surprisingly . . . "MANY PLACES"! Places in the world like France, and I'm married to a Frenchman who always closes bathroom doors.

Where in the World?

While living in the United States a few years ago, I brought up the "potty talk" and cultural differences at our "Oasis of Cultures" (international community group) that met several times a month. In talking to my

European and Indian friends, I discovered that many countries outside the good 'ole USA close the bathroom doors when not in use.

Perhaps this is why . . . **"In North America (especially in the USA), it is quite common to leave bathroom and/or toilet doors ajar when the room is not in use. It tells one at a glance whether the bathroom is occupied. In many European homes, however, the tradition is to keep bathroom doors securely closed at all times. I think this is probably a heritage from the days when 'water closets' were malodorous places and one sought to keep unpleasant odors out of the rest of the house."** —Merry Andrew

In all of our homes in France, we had separate *"W.C." (British origin —"Water Closets"),* with nothing in the small room besides a flush toilet and, sometimes, a tiny handwashing sink. This was a completely separate room from the "bathroom" *(salle de bains)* where you would have a larger sink(s), bathtub, and/or shower. It is even quite common to find a washer and dryer in a European "bathroom," and even a *"bidet."*

It suddenly occurred to me that this is probably the reason many modern, public *"W.C."* in Europe now have lock dials that show "red" for "occupied" and "green" for "unoccupied." It spares people from waiting impatiently outside an unoccupied W.C. Actually, I think I have seen these red and green dials on *"porta-potties"* in the U.S. Those doors must stay closed to contain the odors!

Oops! Language Blooper!

An American friend told me a story about his recent trip to France. He walked proudly into a restaurant, with his carefully formed French sentence, and asked, *"Où est la salle de bains?"* ("Where is the bathroom?")

The man behind the bar looked at him puzzled and made a gesture of "washing under his armpits" and asked him if he needed a shower.

The American tourist laughed and said, "No! Pee-Pee!"

The bartender exclaimed, "Ah, les toilettes?!" That's another word for *"le W.C."*

Don't forget—when traveling in Europe, the toilet door will surely be closed. However, there's a good chance that NO ONE is in there! Just make sure to knock!

Let's Weave Cultures!

Why do you think some cultures keep the W.C. door closed when it's not in use? To keep the unpleasant odors contained? Because the potty is considered "dirty"? Because the potty is considered "private"? Out of cultural habit or tradition?

In your culture or country, do you keep the W.C. door opened or closed when it's not in use? Why?

Merry Andrew—"Bathroom Door Etiquette"— https://able2know.org/ topic/136816-1

Chapter Twenty-Seven
Compliments and Unexpected Gifts!

"With languages, you are at home anywhere." –
Edward De Waal

Shortly after arriving in Morocco, we were thrilled to be invited to our neighbors' home for tea one Sunday afternoon. We had been hoping that we would have opportunities like this to meet local people, taste authentic food, and experience the Moroccan culture up close and personal. Gladly accepting the invitation, I prepared a traditional French cake to take with us—not wanting to arrive at their home empty-handed.

Welcomed In!

Our friendly neighbors welcomed us inside their house for sweet Moroccan mint tea and yummy pastries covered in sticky honey. Pure delight! After having tea, I excused myself to go to the restroom. On my way there, I noticed a beautiful teal green rug. It was gorgeous!

In an awkward blend of French, Arabic, and English, I spurted out, "Your rug is absolutely beautiful!"

Upon exiting the restroom, I noticed the rug again. Overwhelmed by its vivid colors, I couldn't help but say something.

My Favorite Color!

"That teal green is gorgeous! That's my favorite color!"

The hostess nodded her head in agreement and delight. I went on and on about that rug that I loved. We had very few house furnishings. A rug like that would look beautiful in our home.

I Want One!

"Where did you find that beautiful rug? I would love to have one for our new house." I said to my neighbor.

She explained to me that they had just returned from a pilgrimage to Mecca. They had purchased the rug during their trip as a memory of this very important step in their spiritual journey as Muslims.

"Wow!" I said.

A few hours later, not wanting to overstay our welcome, we headed towards the door. Our boys were getting very impatient with the visit, even though they had enjoyed drinking an entire teapot full of sweet Moroccan mint tea and devouring pastries of all shapes and sizes.

My neighbor reached out her hands to me. She was holding a bag. I looked inside the bag and couldn't believe my eyes! The beautiful teal green rug from Saudia Arabia was carefully folded up.

Embarrassed!

Shame and embarrassment flooded my heart and mind. I felt the rush of heat as my face turned beet red. With my eyes about ready to pop out of their sockets, I apologized over and over to my neighbor.

"Oh no, I am so sorry. I cannot take your rug. It's beautiful, but it is your rug."

"You must take my rug," she said. "You love my rug, and it's your favorite color. It will be beautiful in your new house. If you don't take it, I will be very offended. You must accept my gift."

I didn't know what to do. Would I offend her more if I took the rug or if I refused it?

We stood uncomfortably at the door for what seemed like an eternity. She insisted several more times that I take her gift. I finally accepted and thanked her. All I wanted to do was run home and hide!

Speechless

"This means so much to me," I said. "I don't know what to say."

I walked home in silence—speechless.

When I got home, I opened the unexpected gift. I took the beautiful teal green rug from Saudia Arabia out of the bag. I laid it on the floor and admired it. It looked beautiful in my new home!

I learned that day to be very careful in how I complimented my Moroccan neighbors and friends.

Recently, I was reading a book called *Do's and Taboos Around the World*. For Morocco, it says, "You may wish to avoid lavishly complimenting your host on a possession, as he may feel socially obligated to give it to you."

Yep! That's right! I will never do that again . . . unless I'm really desperate to furnish my house!

Let's Weave Cultures!

Have you ever made a cultural mistake that led to much shame and embarrassment? How did you handle it when you realized what you had done or said? Were the local hosts understanding of your cultural mistake and blooper or were they offended?

What other *Dos and Taboos Around the World* have you learned?

Do you know other cultures, like Morocco, where a host would feel socially obligated to give you something if you complimented him on it?

Chapter Twenty-Eight
Why Did You Put the Rug There?!

As I pulled the beautiful teal green rug out of the plastic bag, I still felt shame and embarrassment. My new Moroccan neighbor had felt culturally and socially obligated to give me her treasured object. I had complimented her over and over on its beauty and color. I even told her I would love to have the same one for my new home.

Well, here it was in my hands. I had the exact same one for my new house. My neighbor's prized rug from Mecca was now mine.

I made a huge cultural blooper that day and learned a hard cultural lesson that I would never forget!

"The Perfect Spot"

The rug was absolutely stunning, I had to admit. The only thing I needed now was the perfect spot for it in my house.

It wasn't a large rug, so I thought it would look nice in a hallway or small entrance area. I really wanted to show it off—display it in a location where every guest could see it. I didn't want anyone to miss it!

As I looked around my barren and undecorated house, I thought about the guest bathroom. It would look perfect in there—bringing a splash of vivid color to a drab place. The bright, teal green color would "pop" against the white marble floors and green and white tiles.

I proudly laid it on the center of my bathroom floor in front of the double sink. Every guest would see it and parade upon it.

No One Would Miss It!

A few days later, one of my Moroccan friends came over for a visit.

At one point, she excused herself to go to the bathroom. I knew my friend would notice my new bathroom rug. Surely, she would like it as much as I did.

Upon exiting, she asked me why I had a "prayer rug" in my bathroom.

"What?! A prayer rug!?" I was so embarrassed. I didn't know that this beautiful, teal green rug from Mecca was a prayer rug.

A Cultural Lesson: "*Hashek!*"

A bathroom, with a toilet, is not considered a clean place in Arab culture. It is "*Hashek*," as we say in Morocco—certainly not a place where you would roll out your prayer mat and talk to God. It was the last place you would have a sacred prayer rug!

I was so ashamed! "*Hashek!*"

I explained to my friend what had happened at my neighbor's house a few days before. We both laughed hysterically!

That day, I learned a few more valuable cultural lessons—how to identify "prayer rugs" and where NOT to place them.

Thankfully, my dear friend had the courage to tell me about my cultural mistake.

What if my next-door neighbor had come over for mint tea, only to find her blessed "gift" on my dirty bathroom floor?!

Let's Weave Cultures!

Have you ever made a cultural mistake that led to much shame and embarrassment? How did you handle it when you realized what you had done or said? Were the local hosts understanding of your cultural mistake and blooper, or were they offended?

What other "Dos and Taboos Around the World" have you learned?

Do's and Taboos Around the World—Roger Axtell—
https://able2know.org/topic/136816-1

Chapter Twenty-Nine

There are Objects Hidden From the GPS!

"The limits of my language are the limits of my world."

— Ludwig Wittgenstein

As usual, while living in the United States a few years ago, my husband, Vincent, plugged the address into the GPS to determine our time of departure from the house. Our destination was 1h15 away, and the roads were all clear. We scheduled to leave accordingly, giving ourselves fifteen minutes of buffer time in case we ran into any unexpected traffic. We were right on schedule for our event starting at 9 a.m. It even looked like we would arrive early. Perfect, just like Vincent likes it—early.

Early, it seemed, until we hit traffic. Major traffic! Going through the mountain hills, we suddenly found ourselves crawling behind a long line of vehicles on the narrow two-lane road.

What's the Hold Up?!

What could be the holdup? The GPS continued to show all roads clear, with no signs of traffic.

Little by little, we saw the cars go around a slow-moving object near the side of the road. In the distance, we could see something black. What was it?

As we approached the dark object, nearing our turn to go around it, we realized what the holdup was. It was an Amish horse and buggy, slowly galloping along. It wasn't just one carriage. Rather, it was one carriage after another. Multiple lines of traffic were backed up to pass by them.

Cultural Awareness—AGAIN!

Our eyes were suddenly opened to the world around us. This was another wake up call in cultural awareness!

As we looked at our GPS, we realized that our GPS had not taken into consideration the Amish horses and buggies in the hills of rural Pennsylvania. They obviously could not be detected by satellite. We live in "Amish country," so this must happen to a lot of drivers.

By the end of our journey, we ended up being fifteen minutes late to our event, not fifteen minutes early!

While living in the "Land Between," our family has found several cultural games. Besides playing "Counting Camo," our family can now play "Counting Carriages"!

Let's Weave Cultures!

What unexpected traffic have you come across during your travels? Flight, train, and bus delays? In Morocco, we often ran into moped accidents, camel crossings, broken donkey carts...

Chapter Thirty
Is the Circus Really Coming to Town?

S everal times a week, early in the morning—around 9:30 a.m.—it sounds like the circus is coming to town. Or, perhaps it is the local fish and vegetable vendors announcing what produce they have for sale. Or, perhaps it is the ice cream truck making its early morning rounds in the neighborhood.

Someone is trying to wake everyone up in Spain. Someone is trying to get everyone's attention.

I observed from the window. It was a large white truck with a blaring intercom attached to the roof. It repeated over and over the same message.

More Language Barriers!

There was a major language barrier standing between me and the speaker's words, so I wasn't exactly sure what was being said.

Our family was used to language and cultural barriers—at drive-thrus, in parking lots, at grocery stories, with grandparents, at Dairy Queen . . .

After all, "I Learned My Spanish in Zumba Class," so I was still quite limited in my Spanish language skills!

Having breakfast on our back porch in the early morning hours, my husband, Vincent, and I were always close to the action—close to the white truck and its blaring speaker. What was it?

It Sounded Like . . .

It sounded like an announcement for the circus coming to town—declaring loudly that parents and their children needed to buy tickets for the upcoming show. It sounded like the local fish and vegetable vendors in Morocco who would ride their donkey carts through the neighborhood streets—shouting in Arabic that they had fresh produce ready to be delivered to your front door. Very handy! It sounded like the ice cream man —inviting children to come to the truck to choose their favorite flavor of ice cream displayed on the vivid images of the truck's side panel.

I'm not sure if they still have ice cream trucks in America, but it was certainly one highlight of my childhood. I can still remember hearing the bells ringing in the distance. Frantically, I would run through the house trying to round up enough loose change to buy my favorite treat.

I was getting excited and searched for some *centimos*! Perhaps there were ice cream trucks in Spain. Who can't eat ice cream at 9:30 a.m.?

I wondered what this man's announcement was in Spanish and what in the world was in his large, white truck. It circled around our neighborhood regularly.

A Mystery

It was a mystery.

One day, an expat friend came over for a visit. She had been living in Spain for three years and spoke Spanish. Perfect timing! The truck's speaker began wailing and calling out to the world.

"What is that?!" I asked my friend. "Is it the circus coming to town, the neighborhood vegetable vendor, or the local ice cream truck?!"

"None of those," she answered with a chuckle. "It's a company announcing that they will pick up any household items that you no longer want. It doesn't matter what condition they are in, they will take them away for you. They fix them up and resell them."

"Wow!" I said. "What a great community recycling plan! That's certainly handy. It's like having the weekly Goodwill or Salvation Army truck come by your house to haul off all your unwanted belongings!"

I have to confess that I was disappointed that it wasn't the circus truck, nor the fish vendor, nor the ice cream man.

I better get used to the loudspeaker announcement. The truck will come down the street again in a few days. Maybe I better go through my storage and round up some unwanted and unneeded items for them to haul away!

Let's Weave Cultures!

Have you ever been exposed to something new in a foreign culture that you couldn't understand because of a language barrier? Did you naturally compare it to something familiar from your own culture? How did you solve the mystery?

Chapter Thirty-One
Awkward Greetings—Kiss or Not?

"Language is the road map of a culture. It tells
you where its people come from and where they
are going." – Rita Mae Brown

Greetings—they can be so awkward, especially when moving to a foreign country. You simply don't know what to do. You don't know what is culturally appropriate.

Upon arriving in our small town in Spain, our American friends introduced our neighbors to us. Our "expat" friends had been living in Spain for five years, and they seemed to know what they were doing.

We met the mother of the family that day. My American friend kissed her, so I did the same—kissing the Spanish woman on either cheek—starting with the right side. It seemed comfortable and "correct."

The next day, while with my same American friend, we saw the same neighbor lady walking on the other side of the street.

"*Hola,*" my friend said to the Spanish woman.

"*Hola,*" she responded.

That was it! No "How are you doing?" No walking across the street to give her kisses. Nothing more than "*hola*" from afar.

I was shocked.

"I noticed you didn't go over and greet her with kisses," I said to my American friend.

"No, because we were on opposite sides of the street and busy doing other things—getting out of the car, walking," she responded.

So Different From France!

Wow! This was so different from France. If you passed your neighbor friend on the street—even if on opposite sides—you would typically stop, greet them with kisses, talk a bit, and then part ways.

Boy, we sure had a lot to learn about Spanish culture!

I had noticed during our evening walks (*paseos*) throughout the neighborhood that no one greeted each other on the streets. There seemed to be no real eye contact and no "*hola*."

"When in Rome, do as the Romans do."

Ok, we will try!

Children are Like Sponges

In the meantime, Pierre, our six-year-old, had become friends with our neighbor's son. The family regularly invited Pierre over to swim, to go on walks with their family, and to play in the park.

Pierre was definitely learning Spanish faster than the rest of us, as he was being fully immersed in the language and culture with his Spanish friends.

When it comes to languages, children are like sponges.

When I dropped Pierre off at our neighbors' driveway to play, I just waved to the neighbors at the door and said "*Hola, Gracias!*" with my limited Spanish vocabulary. When they brought him back to our house, they would say, "*Hola, Bueno, Adios.*"

There were no other greetings, no kisses.

What Do I Do?

One day, as we were unloading groceries in front of our garage door, our neighbors were walking out of their front gate—on their way to the park.

"*Hola*," I said.

"*Hola*," they replied.

I didn't know what to do.

Should I greet them appropriately—whatever that means—since we were standing on the SAME side of the street? Should I kiss them, shake their hands, or just stand there awkwardly and talk to them?

Every country and culture where we have lived is different.

In the south of France, where we last lived, you shake hands first. When you get to know someone well, you kiss twice on the cheeks. In my husband's village in the north of France, you kiss four times. In other regions of France, you kiss three times. In Morocco, I kiss the women, but not the men. In other countries, you kiss, but you start on the opposite cheek.

It can be really confusing.

What should I do? Nothing? Something?

A million cultural questions flooded my mind.

This was the first time I was seeing the father of the family and their two sons up close and personal.

I had to think and act fast. There was no time to run and get my *Culture Shock!—Spain* book and look up how to greet Spanish neighbors.

It felt awkward to not greet them, so I leaned over and kissed the Spanish woman twice on the cheeks—starting with the right side. I didn't want to kiss her and not the rest of the family. That might offend them.

So, I leaned over and kissed the father. We exchanged names while we kissed. I then kissed the two little boys. They seemed somewhat awkward. They turned their heads a bit, so I ended up kissing their foreheads!

Awkward!

We stood there talking for a while, and they extended an invitation for Pierre to go with their family to the park. He immediately accepted, with great enthusiasm.

As we talked, I kept saying to myself, "Did I just do the right thing? Was kissing their entire family culturally appropriate? Did I offend them? Maybe I shouldn't have kissed my neighbor's husband."

I just wasn't sure. They didn't appear offended. I was the one who seemed uncomfortable.

As soon as we parted ways, I grabbed my phone and texted my American friend on Whatsapp. I told her what had happened and asked her if I had just made a major cultural mistake, a major *"faux pas."*

She reassured me that it was fine, since the family had opened up to me. We had been getting to know each other through our children's friendship.

Vincent also encouraged me by saying, "They know that you are an American. They will excuse your behavior and cultural mistakes."

I still didn't know if what I had done was right. I still didn't know what I'd do the next time I crossed paths with my neighbors on the SAME side of the street or on the OPPOSITE side of the street.

How Do I Know What To Do?

Thankfully, I have found several excellent books to help me. *Dos and Taboos Around the World* has been a great resource, as well as *Culture Shock! Spain* to help guide me through this cultural learning maze.

This is what *Culture Shock!—Spain* says about "Kissing."

"Expect a handshake when you are being introduced but do not be surprised if you get kissed on both cheeks when you leave a party or any social gathering."

Maybe I should have just extended my hand to greet the father and the kids, since it was a first introduction. I honestly didn't know.

My Son Knows More Than Me

Thankfully, that's what my older son did.

While I was still talking to the neighbors, after I kissed them all, Robert got out of the car and passed by. I introduced my son to them, and he appropriately shook hands with the mother and the father.

My nineteen-year-old was much more in tune with cross-cultural etiquette than I was. Maybe he could teach his culturally awkward mother a few lessons about Spain!

Two days later . . .

Our neighbors invited us to walk with them to the local park to watch a children's puppet show. We gladly accepted!

When I saw them, I didn't know what to do. Should I kiss them again, or should I greet them from afar?

I chose the latter option and greeted them with a simple *"Hola."*

During the puppet show, our neighbor who speaks English was talking to us about the Spanish culture and the puppet tradition. It was fascinating.

She clearly wanted to be a language and culture teacher for us.

Just Ask!

I just had to ask. I needed to be a "cultural learner."

"What is the best way to greet someone in Spain?" I asked my neighbor. "When I saw you two days ago on the street in front of our house, I didn't know what to do. I kissed you, your husband, and your children. I hope that I didn't offend anyone."

"No, not at all!" she replied with a chuckle. "We don't usually kiss foreigners, because we know that they aren't used to that."

"What about the Spanish?" I asked. "What do they do? We want to greet like the local people here—the Spaniards."

"They kiss!" she exclaimed. "And if I introduce you to our friends, you would kiss them too."

Well, the mystery is solved. Do I kiss or not? KISS—definitely KISS!

As we parted ways that evening after the puppet show, we ALL kissed each other goodbye—except the men! We also took the time to show our new Spanish neighbors how we hug each other in America and how we kiss each other in the north of France—FOUR TIMES!

We all got some good laughs and some good cultural lessons.

So, remember, when in Spain, do you kiss or not? KISS—definitely KISS! Unless there's a global pandemic going on!

Let's Weave Cultures!

Have you ever traveled to a foreign country and didn't know how to greet properly in that culture? What did you do? How did you feel? How did you learn what was culturally appropriate or not?

Chapter Thirty-Two

Kissing Culture—Left or Right?

My husband, Vincent, and I went to our first Spanish lesson at a local tapas bar. We had met a really nice young Spanish woman at a restaurant a few weeks before. I had exchanged phone numbers with her, and we had been texting regularly. Vincent and I wanted to learn Spanish, so we asked her if she could help tutor us once or twice a week.

When we arrived at the tapas bar for our first lesson, our Spanish tutor wasn't there yet. We waited for about ten minutes, and then she finally arrived and approached the table.

Vincent and I weren't really sure how to greet her. We didn't know her very well, so we were clueless what was culturally appropriate in this context.

I took a risk, stood up, and leaned over to kiss her twice on either cheek—starting with the right side. Vincent then did the same thing. However, he didn't start on the right side. He started on the left side! That made for a very uncomfortable greeting as they almost met in the middle—kissing on the lips!

Oops!

This has happened to me on more than one occasion while kissing a man in France. Depending on the region, you start on different sides of your cheeks.

This is definitely one of those cultural questions that you want to ask a local upon arriving in a new foreign "kissing culture." You need to make sure you know what side to start the kisses on!

In Spain, Vincent learned the hard way. Kissing starts on the right side—not the left—and certainly not in the middle . . . unless, of course, he is kissing me!!!!!

Let's Weave Cultures!

Have you ever been to a "kissing culture" and didn't know how to do it? Maybe you didn't know which side to start on or how many times to kiss. How did you eventually figure out the culturally appropriate greeting ritual?

Part 5

Unintentional Vulgarity

WARNING: THIS SECTION CONTAINS STORIES OF 'UNINTENTIONAL VULGARITY.' THERE IS LANGUAGE AND CONTENT INAPPROPRIATE FOR YOUNGER READERS. PARDON, MY FRENCH!

Chapter Thirty-Three

The Sandwich Order We Will Never Forget!

"Keep your language. Love its sounds, its
modulation, its rhythm. But try to march
together with men of different languages, remote
from your own, who wish like you for a more just
and human world."

—Hélder Câmara

WARNING: Some words in this story may be offensive to some readers or not suitable for a younger audience. *"Pardon my French!"*

My husband's first trip to visit me and my family in America was full of hilarious language and cultural bloopers.

Vincent had been studying English since middle school, when it was a requirement in the French educational system. However, like many language classes, the focus was on grammar and writing—rather than on much-needed oral communication. He still had a lot to learn about speaking English!

First Family Outing

Growing up in Missouri, one of our family's favorite restaurants was *Tippin's Pie Factory*. It was also the first place that I worked as a teenager. We couldn't wait to take Vincent there for some traditional meatloaf, chicken pot pie, honey butter cornbread, and the largest variety of pies anyone has ever seen!

Our first meal out to the restaurant was with my mother and my grandparents. It took me a while to translate the entire menu into French for Vincent. It took an even longer time for him to decide what he wanted to eat. There was an overwhelming amount of choices, and he wanted to try them all!

When the impatient server came around a third time to finally take our orders, we were all ready. Vincent wanted to order on his own. He wanted to practice his English.

His First Spoken Words—Oops!

Going around the table in order, it was Vincent's turn. He proudly opened his mouth and spoke in his charming French accent.

"I will take a triple-dicker sandwich," he said cheerfully to the girl with the pad of paper and pen in her hand.

We all broke out laughing. And of course, Vincent had no earthly idea why. With my eyes popping out of my head and a held-back chuckle, I corrected his order with the server.

"He'll take a triple-decker sandwich, please."

When I turned to Vincent to translate into French what had just happened and what he had just said, he was horrified! His face turned bright red with embarrassment in the presence of my older and respectable family members.

Thankfully, his shame quickly turned to laughter. We all had some tears and a good bellyache from laughing so hard.

Vincent's American debut certainly impressed everyone. That is one sandwich description that our family will never forget. I don't think the server will forget either!

Before ordering his slice of pie, Vincent wisely practiced his English pronunciation in my ear.

P.S. My computer continually wants to auto-correct "triple-dicker" to "triple-decker." ("Pardon my French!")

For non-American readers, a "triple-decker" sandwich is a sandwich made of three layers.

Let's Weave Cultures!

What language and cultural bloopers have you made? Tell us your funny (and "not so funny") stories.

How do you keep a humble attitude while learning a new language and culture? How do you respond when people laugh at you when you are learning a foreign language?

Chapter Thirty-Four

Who Hunts for Thongs in the Kitchen Sink?

L iving with a non-native English speaker is filled with fun and laughter. In our home, we live across languages, across cultures, and across borders. It is fun and highly recommended!

The other night, my husband, Vincent, had prepared a nice dinner for us, and we were all gathered at the dining room table.

He wasn't coming to the table just yet. I could hear him rummaging in the sink, moving around the pile of dirty dishes.

"Where are the thongs?!" he yelled out.

"The thongs?" I answered, laughing. "What in the world are you talking about?"

He opened the kitchen drawer and pulled out a pair of tongs. He brought them over to the table to show me.

"Thongs! You know, thongs!" Vincent exclaimed, with a bit of frustration in his voice.

By this time, I was laughing hysterically.

"Those are TONGS, not THONGS!" I said.

"Do you know what THONGS are?" I asked Vincent.

By this time, he had realized the humor in the moment.

"Yes, underwear!" he responded with a smile.

"Yes, and also the sandals with the thing that goes between your toes," I explained.

We laughed together and sat down to enjoy our meal.

What Kind of Blooper is This?

Now, we have to ask ourselves—is this a vocabulary blooper or a pronunciation blooper?

In the French language, there is no "th" sound, as in English. For example, *thé* (tea) is pronounced *"tay"* in French. The name *"Théodore"* is pronounced *"Tay-o-dore."*

Maybe in the end, Vincent had become "over-Anglicized" in his pronunciation—thinking that every "t" is pronounced "th"!

In any case, don't go hunting for a pair of thongs in the kitchen sink! You probably won't find them.

Let's Weave Cultures!

What language and cultural bloopers have you made? Tell us your funny (and "not so funny") stories.

How do you keep a humble attitude while learning a new language and culture? How do you respond when people laugh at you when you are learning a foreign language?

Chapter Thirty-Five

The Shocking Invitation to Spanish Culture!

"We should learn languages because language is the only thing worth knowing even poorly." –
Katy Lomb

A few years ago, before leaving the U.S., we went out to lunch with some dear friends.

Upon entering the restaurant, I said, "The next time we have lunch, it will be in Spain. We'll take you to a *tapas* bar."

I saw a look of surprise and confusion on our friend's face.

Perhaps it was a cultural misunderstanding.

"Do you know what Spanish *tapas* are?"

I gave him a brief explanation. Relief and color quickly returned to his face.

"Oh, I thought you said, 'We will take you to a topless bar,'" our friend said, chuckling.

We all laughed hysterically and wondered curiously if they perhaps have topless, *tapas* bars in Spain.

Let's Weave Cultures!

Do you know what Spanish *"tapas"* are?

"A tapas is an appetizer or snack in Spanish culture and translates to a small portion of any kind of Spanish cuisine. Tapas may be cold (such as mixed olives and cheese) or hot (such as chopitos, which are battered, fried, baby squid). In some bars and restaurants in Spain and across the globe, tapas have evolved into a more sophisticated cuisine. Tapas can be combined to make a full meal." — *Wikipedia [1]*

Try tapas sometime, and make sure you don't forget your swimsuit top!

[1] https://en.wikipedia.org/w/index.php?search=spanish+tapas&title= Special%3ASearch&go=Go&ns0=1

Chapter Thirty-Six

Sometimes It's Best NOT to Ask Questions

Questions . . . I love to ask questions, to explore and discover new things. I'm naturally curious, and I like to understand—especially when it comes to language and culture. I believe we need to be "cultural learners," to ask questions, so we can become culturally aware. Questions usually result in answers. Sometimes, however, the answers can be shocking!

Freebies?

We were recently at a tapas bar with a group of friends. We weren't sure why, but the server told us that all the women would receive a complimentary drink at the end of our meal. Perhaps it was because we were a rather large group, and a lot of money was being spent on the food. The server brought out stemmed glasses filled with a beautiful pink "layered" drink. It looked like a cocktail, but I wasn't sure.

Out of Curiosity

Out of curiosity, I asked the server, "What is it?" in a mix of English and broken Spanish. I didn't want to drink this mysterious Spanish concoction without knowing what I was tasting—what I was enjoying. To help us cross over our language barrier, the server grabbed a menu off the table. He pointed to a photo of a fancy cocktail, and then pointed to its name underneath. I was expecting a beautifully exotic Spanish name.

I read it, and said, "Oh my!" with embarrassment and laughter. I think I even blushed.

Seeing my surprising reaction, two of the ladies in our group, sitting at the end of the table, yelled, "What is it?! What is it?!"

"Sex on the Beach!!" I screamed back.

We all burst out laughing! The server smiled with delight.

Our friends from the U.S. said, "That will surely be something to write home about."

The men in our group were as surprised as we were—speechless even! They wondered why they didn't get the yummy cocktails, too. Feeling bad, some of us shared ours with our husbands.

We still don't understand why ONLY the women at our table were offered the cocktail—and not the men. Perhaps it has a cultural meaning that we will never understand. I didn't ask the server, "Why?" and I don't think I ever will. Sometimes, you just don't want to know. Sometimes, it's best NOT to ask questions!

Let's Weave Cultures!

Have you ever asked a question and got a shocking response? Did you wish you had never asked the question? How did you handle it?

Chapter Thirty-Seven
Do You Know What a 'Fanny Pack' is?

*"We may have different religions, different
languages, different colored skin, but we all
belong to one human race."* —Kofi Annan

**(WARNING: Some words in this story may be offensive to some readers
or not suitable for a younger audience. *"Pardon my French!"*)**

One day, I traveled to visit my son who was studying in England—the one I
released to the other side of the world.

As soon as I arrived in the U.K., I heard the accents. These British accents are
strangely familiar to me and sparked a lot of fun memories.

Living in the south of France for seven years, we were surrounded by the
British. The Airbus industry attracted many from across the Channel. As a
result, our boys were in the "British section" of their French middle school
and high school—taught by wonderful British teachers. Our boys came out
speaking British English—even though they were American!

We had a lot of British friends at school, at church, at the gym, and in our
English Café.

Our local church hosted an English conversation group every other week,
where people from around the world could come to learn and practice
English. Those who led the conversation time were American and British.

Sometimes, our expressions and vocabulary choices differed and led to some interesting conversation topics.

I'll never forget the day when I led a discussion about travel." I was explaining to the participants that sometimes people will carry a backpack or a fanny pack, a small bag that attaches around your waist. As soon as I said "fanny pack," my British friends gasped out loud.

What Did I Say?!

"What did I say?" I wondered.

"Don't say 'fanny pack'!" one lady exclaimed.

"Why?" I asked, a bit puzzled.

"Do you know what a 'fanny' is?" she asked me.

"Yeah, your backside or bottom," I said innocently.

"NOT IN BRITISH ENGLISH!" she said with a lot of intensity.

I could tell that she was embarrassed, as she tried to explain and awkwardly show, with gestures, the meaning of this word.

It was hard for me to understand what she was trying to discreetly show me. Finally, she just said it.

"A 'fanny' is a 'vagina'!" she screamed. She explained that it is even more vulgar than that.

"Oh, my goodness!" I said, laughing. "So does that mean that a 'fanny pack' is a 'sanitary napkin'?!"

I wondered if the equivalent of a "fanny pack" even existed in England, and if so, what was it called?

Afterwards, I did some research—fanny packs were called "bum bags." This makes sense, because the equivalent of "fanny" in American English is "bum" in British English.

Just to be safe, I didn't bring my "fanny pack" with me to England to visit my son!

Let's Weave Cultures!

Have you ever used a word with an entirely different meaning in another country or culture? How did you find out the meaning?

Chapter Thirty-Eight

It's Not a Rubber!

(**WARNING: Some words in this story may be offensive to some readers or not suitable for a younger audience.** *"Pardon my French!"*)

I'm not vulgar, or at least I like to believe that I'm not. However, being in England a few years ago flooded my mind with funny memories of language bloopers. I'm not sure why, but language bloopers often have a bit of vulgar humor in them—at least many of mine do. I think that's what makes them "bloopers" and so funny. My apologies, in advance.

A Unique Program

As I mentioned in "Do You Know What a 'Fanny Pack' is?", our seven years in the southwest of France brought us in regular contact with British citizens. Most of them worked for Airbus.

Our four boys were enrolled in a public French school that had a "British Section" for bi-lingual children. It was a program subsidized by the Airbus industry to aid English-speaking families working in the region. This unique program allowed our children to remain completely fluent in English while still learning French and integrating into the national educational system.

Our boys were American, and we spoke American English at home. On the other hand, all of their English teachers at school were British—not American. As a result, our children learned British English, not American English.

A Drastic Difference!

I first discovered the drastic difference between British and American English when I first taught English in a high school in the south of France. This high school had only had British English teachers in the past. I was the first American to teach at their high school through the Fulbright Teaching Fellowship. From my first day of work, the administration informed me I needed to teach the students British English, not American English.

"I am not British," I told the school director. "I am an American. I speak American English. I have been sent here by the U.S. Government."

Hours were spent trying to learn British vocabulary and how to tell time. I practiced and then taught "Half-past two" rather than "2:30." It was a challenge.

There are many differences in vocabulary and expressions between the two languages. They are truly two distinct languages!

This became a reality in our home, when our boys would walk through the door from school speaking with a British accent and using British English vocabulary.

Strange Words in Our Home

They called their friends "mates" and their mother "Mum," and used "bloody" to emphasize something they were saying. For example, "That was a bloody good football game!"

I can remember David coming home and asking for water from the "tap."

"Oh, the faucet, you mean," I answered with a smile.

Then, there was the day when David was doing his homework at the kitchen table. He was six-years-old.

"Mommy, where's my rubber?" he asked.

I burst out laughing, and it took me a moment to realize what he was referring to.

"Oh, you need a pencil eraser, honey?" I asked with a smile.

"No, I need a rubber, Mummy," David insisted.

"Honey, it's not a rubber in American English. It's an eraser."

I explained to my son that we use different words for certain objects in the United States and in England.

At home, David had an "eraser" at the end of his pencil. At school, he had a "rubber" at the end of his pencil.

This can be quite confusing for a child in the first grade!

A Funny Story . . .

This reminded me of a story that I once heard from a friend.

A British man went to the U.S. to work for an American company. On the first day of his new job, he went into the company director's office and asked where he could find some rubbers. This was shocking to the American businessman! The American's reaction was shocking to the British man!

They eventually figured out the language barrier and laughed about it. The new British employee needed pencil erasers—not condoms! Whew!

Let's Weave Cultures!

Have you ever had to correct a child or someone you know when they used a word that was inappropriate in certain places or contexts? The word was correct, but not in that situation?

Chapter Thirty-Nine
Is it Ok to Have Wet Hair?

"One of the benefits of being bicultural is simply
the awareness that how you live is not the only
way." – Ann Campanella

I was running late for my Spanish lesson. My husband, Vincent, was already waiting for me outside. I jumped out of the shower, threw my wet hair up in a ponytail, and rushed out the door.

As we walked towards the tapas bar to meet our language tutor, I suddenly stopped in my tracks.

"Ugh!" I thought to myself. "What if it's not culturally appropriate in Spain for a woman to go out of her house with wet hair?"

A Strange Question

Now, this may seem like a strange question to ask myself. However, I was a cultural learner, and I needed to know. In all of my reading of *Dos and Taboos Around the World* and *Cultural Shock! Spain*, I had not come across this topic.

Why's that? Probably because no one really thought about it.

But I did, and here's why.

When I was pursuing my Master's degree in Cross-Cultural Studies, I had a professor who had lived and worked in Mali, West Africa for decades. She had told us a story about her family's first days in the village, living along the river.

Mary had beautiful, long, flowing hair that hung down to her knees. She washed her hair often, not every day, but often.

She didn't like to blow dry her hair, and electricity was hit-or-miss and a real luxury in that part of the world. Most days, Mary would shower and then walk around the village, allowing her hair to naturally dry in the scorching sun and breeze.

Why All the Stares?

Mary noticed everyone kept staring at her, her wet hair, and her husband. This went on for days, weeks, and months. Finally, Mary could speak enough of the local dialect that she could ask a simple question to the women.

"Why do you look at me and my husband every time I come out of the house with wet hair? I don't understand."

Mary was a cultural learner. She was living in a foreign land, learning a new language, and living among people different from her. Mary and her husband took risks and asked questions, so they could learn, so their eyes could be open to the world around them. They didn't want to live in that place, among those people, in ignorance. Mary and her husband wanted to know, to learn, to understand, to adapt, to integrate . . .

Mary wanted to cultivate her cultural awareness, and she did it by asking questions to the locals in her community.

That day, she finally asked the question. She just had to know.

She Had to Know—Cultural Awareness!

"Why do you look at me and my husband every time I come out of the house with wet hair? I don't understand," she asked the women as they walked together to the village market.

The women were uncomfortably silent. Finally, one of the local women dared to open her mouth and respond to Mary's cultural question.

"Women only wash their hair after having intimate relations with their husband. You and your husband must have intimate relations a lot," said the young woman with her eyes down, embarrassed to speak the words.

Mary was horrified and tried to explain to the women that she washed her hair frequently because of the African dirt. It had nothing to do with her husband!

The women all laughed together!

Horror and Laughter

From that time on, Mary started washing her hair less frequently, and she never walked out of the house until it was completely dry!

I will never forget that story.

As I walked to my Spanish lesson, I wondered what my tutor would think about my wet hair. What would the server say? Would they look at me and my husband with curiosity?

Is it Culturally Appropriate?

When our language helper arrived, I asked her the question.

"Is it culturally appropriate in Spain for me to walk out of my house with wet hair?" I asked her.

She seemed puzzled that I would ask such a strange question.

"No, it's not a problem. Why?" she asked.

"In some cultures, it is a problem," I said. I then told her the story about Mary and the people from Mali.

We all laughed!

Thankfully, it's culturally acceptable here in Spain for a woman or man to walk out of the house with his or her hair still wet.

Good thing! Chances are, I'll be running late to next week's Spanish lesson too—with wet hair!

LET'S WEAVE CULTURES!

Have you ever traveled or lived in a foreign country in which you did something culturally inappropriate—but didn't know? If so, how did you eventually find out?

Chapter Forty

Beware! The Danger of Direct Translation!

T hey call them *"faux amis."*

I can remember learning about them in my high school French class. "Fake friends" or "false friends" are believed to be dangerous in the French language . . . those words that appear to sound alike in both French and English (but aren't). In official grammatical terms, they are called "cognates," in this case, "false cognates."

For example, "television" and *"télévision,"* or "radio" and *"radio,"* or "hotdog" and *"hotdog"* aren't *"faux amis."* They actually represent the same thing in both languages.

"Faux amis," on the other hand, are spelled alike and sound very similar . . . but their meanings are worlds apart! As one can clearly see by the chosen adjective in this expression, the idea of a "false" friend indicates that something about it isn't true or real. Something about it is inaccurate. Perhaps one could call it a false assumption.

Learning the Language

I met my first "fake friend" up close and personal during my first year living abroad in France as a foreign exchange student. Only nineteen-years-old, I lived with a French family in a tiny, picturesque village north of Paris.

My summer job was as a nanny—*au pair*—caring for two adorable children. Thomas was three and wore the cutest blue round glasses. He would correct my pronunciation throughout the entire children's book that I would read to him at bedtime. It was very humbling. Every day, I placed Thomas on the infant seat attached to my bike and rode him back and forth to the village preschool. I also cared for a three-month-old baby girl named Pauline. The day after arriving in France, my French *"Maman,"* Marie-Thérèse, placed her precious little bundle of joy in my arms and walked out the door to work all day. Panicked, I called my mother in the U.S. for advice, as I had never in my life changed a baby's diaper!

Meeting the French Family

In honor of their new American nanny, the French family for whom I worked invited their entire extended family for Sunday lunch. This was a traditional, fancy, sit-down French meal that would last several courses and several hours. I couldn't wait to have this family cultural experience.

In preparation, I worked hard on correctly formulating and practicing one complete sentence I could share with the family during the meal.

Prior to my arrival in France, my language learning had taken place in a classroom. I'm thoroughly convinced now that one cannot learn a foreign language confined within four walls. One must be fully immersed in the language and culture, with no chance of escape, only survival. One must literally be placed in a "sink or swim" situation.

At this point in my journey, my French was basic classroom French. I could construct simple grammatical sentences; however, my vocabulary was quite limited.

Preparation For the Big Moment . . . Direct Translation

Sitting alone in my bedroom the night before the big family meal, I thought long and hard about my big debut with the new relatives. What could I say . . . something that would make me look great, revealing my great language ability and my deep cultural insight?

After minutes, maybe even hours, of pondering, the revelation came to me. At just the right moment during the next day's meal, I would say, "I love French bread, because there are no preservatives."

Perhaps my statement could lead to a more in-depth conversation about the differences between French and American bread. I was so excited! This was the perfect sentence.

Practice Makes Perfect, Right?

I worked hard to translate and write out my sentence. The structure was simple enough.

"I love French bread . . ." That was easy. *"J'aime le pain français . . ."*

The next part also didn't seem too challenging. " . . . because there are no . . ." was translated as " . . . *parce qu'il n'y a pas de . . ."*

After that, I was a bit stumped. I didn't know the French word for "preservatives."

This was in the dinosaur days before the internet and Google Translate, but no worries! I had packed in my suitcase my very heavy and very thick Harrap's French/English dictionary. Thumbing through the "Ps," I couldn't find "preservatives," and it was too expensive to call my college French professor back in the U.S.

I could remember back to my French textbooks and literature books. There was so much crossover between the French and English languages. Many American words had made themselves into the French language, *"hamburger," "jean," "t-shirt."* I was educated and could make an educated guess.

Surely, I could use direct translation!

"Preservatives" in English must be *"préservatifs"* in French . . . same word, just slightly different pronunciation.

Because French had both masculine and feminine noun forms, I had to decide on the gender of my new word, *"préservatifs"* or *"préservatives."* With no rhyme or reason, I made this new noun masculine. It sounded better, more distinguished.

I had it . . . my new and complete sentence. *"J'aime le pain français, parce qu'il n'y a pas de préservatifs."*

I wrote it out and memorized it, practicing it over and over in front of the mirror until I had it down just right. In my sleep that night, I rehearsed it. I was ready for my first French family feast, and they were going to be so impressed!

Ready or Not, Here I Come!

The next day came, and I was delighted to meet *Pépé, Mémé, Tata, Tonton*, and all the little cousins. Their entire family was present that day, and they were as excited to meet the blonde American stranger as I was to meet them.

We enjoyed a gourmet meal with appetizers, lamb, vegetables, salad, cheese, wine, fancy desserts, and of course, delicious and fresh French bread.

I prayed for just the right moment to say my sentence. Waiting and waiting patiently, I built up the courage to open my mouth and let it flow. I found the perfect moment, and I seized it.

"J'aime le pain français, parce qu'il n'y a pas de préservatifs."

There I said it, with such pride and joy. My face was beaming ear to ear with a radiant grin, as I knew that my pronunciation was near perfect. Boy, were they going to be impressed by this American girl!

Something is Wrong!

Then, I realized that something was wrong.

Impressed, they were! I felt the weight of heavy silence. Quiet chuckles slowly broke out around the table, building up into a loud roar from all sides.

At first, I thought they were just extremely impressed with my spoken level of French, my distinguished use of vocabulary, and my fine-tuned pronunciation. Then, I realized that something was wrong.

They were not laughing with me; they were laughing at me. There is a big difference.

I turned to Eric, my French *"Papa,"* who pulled me aside from the table. He explained to me, in his broken English, what a *"préservatif"* was. It was a very awkward moment.

His limited vocabulary didn't allow him to find the exact translation, but I understood enough from his descriptive words and gestures. A *"préservatif"* in French is not at all a "preservative." Rather, it is a "condom!"

I couldn't believe my ears! "That's not what I meant!"

I looked at my French *"Papa"* with eyes as big as saucers, and my mind and heart were filled with horror. This American girl had just made a public proclamation before their entire extended family that "I like French bread because there are no condoms!"

I returned to the table to apologize, *"Pardonnez-moi."* We all laughed together.

That would be the last time I would try to use direct translation when I didn't know a word in French.

I didn't know until then that a "false friend" had also been invited to our big French family Sunday meal!

Let's Weave Cultures!

Do you know any *"faux amis"* ("false friends") in other languages? When and where have you accidentally used them? How did you know you had made a mistake? What did you do when you realized?

Chapter Forty-One

That's Not What I Meant!

"Travel makes one modest, you see what a tiny place you occupy in the world." —Gustave Flaubert

(WARNING: Some words in this story may be offensive to some readers or not suitable for a younger audience. *"Pardon my French!"*)

"'My ass?!' What do you mean, 'my ass'?!" she said with shock on her face.

Language barriers—they cause all kinds of confusion and offense.

Recently, we met some new friends at a café. Well, we call them *"cafés,"* because we are French. Here in Spain, they call them *"bars."* They are ta*pas bars*, and yes, people are ordering and drinking beer in the wee hours of the morning. We were drinking our nice, hot *cafe con leche*.

We were having a fascinating conversation with our new acquaintances— introductions made through mutual friends. It was the first time we were meeting face-to-face, rather than through phone texts.

Our new friends were a bi-cultural couple. The husband was from Morocco, and the wife was from Spain. We flowed naturally in and out of four languages during our conversation—Arabic, French, Spanish, and English.

Weaving Cultures!

That's what I call "Weaving Cultures"! I love it!

Paola was an English teacher in a local high school, so her English was excellent. As a language teacher, however, she was eager to help us learn Spanish as well.

We talked about our lives in Morocco and our favorite places to visit there. They asked us how we were doing with life in Spain and the cultural adjustment and transition. We talked about our desire to learn the Spanish language and culture.

After we finished our *cafe con leche*, we walked across the street to the Wednesday outdoor market.

Her Favorite Vendors

Paola wanted to show me her favorite vendors in the *"mercado de ropas"* (the clothing market). Yeah! This was just what I wanted and needed—an insider's view of the city market. There is nothing better than being shown around by a local from the area—a real native.

Paola showed me her favorite place to buy purses, clothes, shoes, and fabric. She bought a purse for five euros (not bad!), and I picked up some colorful, striped fabric for my dining room table (only three euros). We then passed a stand with women's leggings—only leggings.

"This is the best place to buy leggings," she told me. "They are very cheap."

Practice Makes Perfect

Wanting to practice my Spanish, I looked at the sign over the table of leggings. It said, *"Mallas—3 euros."* I wasn't sure how to pronounce the foreign word. I knew that the *"ll"* in Spanish was pronounced like a *"y."* I gave it my best shot.

"My ass," I said slowly and hesitantly.

Paola looked at me with confusion. She didn't know that I was reading the sign and trying to speak in Spanish. Up to that point, our conversation at the market had been entirely in English.

"*My ass,*" I said, a bit more firmly and loudly, in order for her to hear and to correct my pronunciation. I was obviously getting it wrong, because she couldn't even understand what I was TRYING to say.

"*My ass, my ass, my ass,*" I repeated over and over. Now, I was confused and getting a bit frustrated.

"'*My ass*?!' What do you mean, '*My ass*'?!" Paola said with shock on her face.

"Not '*my ass*' in English," I said. "'*My ass*' in Spanish!" I said, pointing to the sign that said, "*Mallas—3 euros.*"

"I thought you were talking about how good 'my ass' or 'your ass' would look in the leggings!" she said.

A Funny Language Barrier

We both started laughing so hard that tears were streaming down our cheeks and our bellies ached. I thought I might even pee my pants!

The guys wondered what in the world was so funny over at the leggings stand.

We told them the story, and they laughed as hard as we did.

I will NEVER forget the word for leggings in Spanish—"*mallas*" which is pronounced "*myass.*" I just have to say it quickly. It's one word—not two!

LET'S WEAVE CULTURES!

What language and cultural bloopers have you made? Have you ever said something vulgar—accidentally?! Tell us your funny (and "not so funny") stories.

Chapter Forty-Two
Do You Need a 'Napkin' or a 'Serviette'?

D uring one of my life coaching courses, the instructor taught us a practical "napkin exercise" to use with coaching clients. He encouraged us to draw a diagram on a paper napkin during casual conversations in restaurants to engage our clients in reflection and discussion.

When I heard "napkin exercise," I chuckled to myself.

While living in France, I had a lot of British friends. We often discussed vocabulary differences between American English and British English. Several of these conversations revolved around the word "napkin" and its difference in meanings.

Here's a story that I came across recently from an American college student who studied in London.

"I'm a napkin person. At every meal I tend to use a lot of napkins . . . anywhere from 3-5, depending on whether the napkins are the flimsy paper kind or the cloth ones. Out at a restaurant, I never seem to have enough napkins. I always ask for more napkins. While in London, I ate out often, and I noticed that every time I would ask the server for more 'napkins,' I would get funny looks. I felt as if I had asked for something dirty or disgusting. People knew what I meant and always handed me more napkins. But they seemed to give me a weird look.

Why the strange looks?

Who says they speak the same language in Britain? In England, the word 'napkin' is typically used to describe a feminine hygiene product (sanitary napkin). Although most people are aware of the double usage of the word, in London, the word 'serviette' is preferred in a restaurant or eating establishment. I did not find this out until my third week in London when I was attending an orientation meeting for overseas students through the university, and they went over some of the common problems Americans have while in London. Boy, was my face red! Would have been nice to know a tad earlier."

Differing Opinions

Perhaps this type of confusing vocabulary incident could only occur in London. I honestly don't know. There seem to be different opinions among my British friends.

In a recent conversation with my British friend from Bristol, I told her this story and asked her opinion. She said that the British would never use the word "napkin" to refer to a "sanitary pad." Rather, they would use the word "pad." She said that the British know Americans refer to "serviettes" as "napkins," and that it's not a problem.

While traveling in England recently to visit my son—the one I released to the other side of the world, I noticed a sign in the women's bathroom stall. It didn't say "sanitary napkins." Rather, it said, "sanitary towels."

Now, that adds even more confusion to this topic of conversation.

Just to be safe . . . if I am coaching a British client, I will find another name for the "napkin exercise"!

LET'S WEAVE CULTURES!

Poll: What do you think?

1.The British only use the word "napkin" to refer to a "sanitary napkin."

2. The British use the word "napkin" to refer to a paper or cloth table napkin—like Americans.

https://www2.pacific.edu/sis/culture/pub/1.1.1_Activity_The_Iceberghw2.htm

Chapter Forty-Three

My Most Embarrassing Blooper in Spain!

"The world is a book and those who do not travel

read only one page."

—Augustine of Hippo

As you know from my many stories of language bloopers, I have had some whoppers! These linguistic incidents usually end in laughter, smiles, tears . . . and sometimes, some downright embarrassment and shame.

This time, however, ended in horror!

On our way home from the hospital after my son's emergency appendectomy, I swung by the pharmacy for his pain medication. I also needed to get some antiseptic, some sterile gauze, and some bandages to cover his incisions.

That all sounded simple enough.

I went to the pharmacy where I usually go. They are friendly, and the owner speaks English. He is kind and patient, always encouraging me to speak Spanish. Only if we can't get past the language barriers does he break out into English.

After greeting him, I explained my son had just had laparoscopic surgery for appendicitis. I showed him the prescription from the hospital for the pain medication. I then told him I needed some antiseptic, some gauze, and some bandages.

Using my French for a base, I quickly formulated my sentence in Spanish.

"*Nessicito antiseptico, compressas, y bandages,*" I said loudly and clearly. For some reason, when speaking a foreign language, I tend to speak louder than usual. It's as if I think my volume might help others understand me better. That is definitely not the case.

I think the other customers in the pharmacy also heard my request.

I wasn't sure of the word for bandages, but I figured "*bandages*" was close enough. In French, "*bandages*" are more like a wrap for injuries, rather than a bandaid, but I assumed he would understand what I meant.

The tall man behind the counter began laughing and said, "N*o bandages, no bandages!*"

I knew right away that I had used the wrong word. He laughed uncomfortably, so I knew I had probably said something vulgar.

"What does '*bandages*' mean in Spanish?" I asked him in English.

He started laughing even harder and said, "That is a conversation for another day."

"Oh, boy!" I thought to myself. "It's so bad that he can't even tell me."

I had found myself in these types of situations before. I can remember in Morocco, when learning Arabic. We would say something vulgar, but our friends and language tutors were too embarrassed to explain the meaning to us. They would just blush and hide their eyes. In those cases, we never knew what we had said wrong and what it meant. We probably continued to make the same mistake over and over, because we could never correct ourselves!

The pharmacist got me the needed medicine and supplies: pain killers, antiseptic, sterile gauze, and large bandaids.

"I'm going to go to my car now and ask Google what '*bandages*' means in Spanish," I told him after paying. "It must be vulgar."

"Does it have a sexual meaning?" I asked him, blushing.

"It's like a slave," he said.

"A slave? You mean a prostitute," I asked, shocked.

"Just a moment," he said in English. He typed something into his computer keyboard and waited for the image to appear on his screen.

In a perfect British accent, the woman behind me spoke. She had been listening to the conversation.

"'*Bandages*' in Spanish are only used for tying someone up for a sexual act," she said.

"Oh, my goodness!" I said. "I'm so embarrassed. But, I'm glad to know that word so I don't use it again."

We all laughed together, and I quickly said goodbye and ran out of the pharmacy.

When I reached the car, I told my son the story.

"That's hilarious!" he said.

"No, it's not!" I said, "I told him that my son needed *bandages*!"

I had just met another "*faux ami*" in the Spanish language. There are a lot of them out there—in all languages! Be on guard!

LET'S WEAVE CULTURES!

What language and cultural bloopers have you made? Have you ever said something vulgar—accidentally?! How did you find out and how did you handle the shock? Tell us your funny (and "not so funny") stories.

Chapter Forty-Four
Dangerous Two-Letter Words

How can a tiny two-letter word get you in so much trouble?

In the French language, and in many other languages around the world, there are tiny words called "articles." They are carefully placed before a noun and are of utmost importance—even though they are small.

Each of these little articles are assigned a gender. They are either male or female, boy or a girl. There is no neutral, in-between, or mixed gender.

The gender issue around the world is one of confusion, and it is the same with linguistic gender. I, personally, do not see any rhyme or reason, any logic in the minds of the decision makers of language—those who assign the gender to a noun.

For example, help me understand why a car in French is feminine . . . *LA voiture,* rather than *LE voiture*? In my mind, an automobile should be masculine, rather than female. Don't you agree? Nope!

Why is a television feminine, *LA télévision,* while a pen is masculine, *LE stylo*?

In Spanish, why is a hamburger feminine, *LA hamburguesa,* while a chicken is masculine, *EL pollo*?

I can see why a girl is feminine in both languages, *LA fille, LA niña*. It makes sense that a boy is masculine, *LE garçon, EL niño*.

However, most of the time, there is no logical reasoning.

In addition, there are words in French that change meaning ONLY by the article change of masculine and feminine. Now, talk about confusion!

Confusion and danger.

One of these words in the French language is MOULE. If you add the masculine article, LE, then it means a "mold," as in a shape or form. For example, if you want to say, "the cake pan," you say, "*LE moule à gâteau.*" If you want to say, "he fit right in," you would say, "*Il est rentré dans LE moule.*"

That was an expression that I had learned early in my French language learning. However, it wasn't an expression that I used regularly.

One day, I was speaking to my husband, Vincent, about one of our sons and his new school experience. I wanted to tell him he fit right in on the first day of class.

"*Il est rentré dans LA moule.*"

Did you notice what I said? Did you notice I changed the article from masculine to feminine, from *LE* to *LA*?

Perhaps you did, because I put those two tiny words in bold capital letters for you to see. However, I will tell you I did NOT notice that I had made that slight gender change.

Well, my French husband noticed, and he burst out laughing.

"What in the world did I just say"? is always my first question when someone laughs at me while speaking a foreign language.

It took my husband a few minutes to regain his composure before explaining to me the giant language "*faux pas*" I had just made.

He patiently explained to me that *LE moule* is different from *LA moule*. They have extremely different meanings.

LE moule means the mold, the form, the shape. *LA moule* means the mussel —as in the shellfish. However, when you use the expression, "*Il est rentré dans LA moule,*" it actually means, "He entered the vagina." I don't need to say more.

"We have to tell all the other language learners on our team!" I told Vincent. "They could so easily make this same '*faux pas*,' and they don't have a French husband to correct them. Their friends and acquaintances might not have the courage to explain the difference and translate the expression."

These tiny two-letter words can be dangerous! So, when you are learning a language that has masculine and feminine articles, beware! Don't get sucked into gender confusion—it can get you into a lot of trouble!

LET'S WEAVE CULTURES!

What language and cultural bloopers have you made? Have you ever said something vulgar—accidentally?! How did you find out and how did you handle the shock? Tell us your funny (and "not so funny") stories.

Chapter Forty-Five
The Bible Story 'Oops'

"The real voyage of discovery consists not in seeking new landscapes, but in having new eyes." —Marcel Proust

I love to share stories, especially Bible stories.

During our first year in North Africa, I went to visit my best friend, Aicha, for a glass of sweet mint tea and *m'simmon* pastries smothered in melted butter and honey.

"Please tell me another story," she said one day as she kneeled at my feet doing elaborate henna designs on my ankles.

I had been studying Arabic intensively, but I was far from being fluent. My accent, especially, was far from native-speaker standards.

In the Arabic language, you must be careful. If you make a slight change in intonation of a word, sometimes, you can end up saying a very different word with a very different meaning.

That day, I decided to tell Aicha the story of creation and Adam and Eve. As I began the story, Aicha lowered her gaze and smiled timidly. Little by little, she broke out into a quiet chuckle.

"Oh boy! What did I say?" I asked her.

She was clearly too embarrassed to tell me, but I insisted.

"You have to tell me what I said. If not, I'll continue to make the same shameful mistake," I said, laughing.

In a whisper, she carefully explained to me that there were two almost identical words in Arabic—the word for "Eve" and the word for "sex." It was only the intonation that changed slightly to drastically change the meaning.

I quickly recalled my storyline and realized that I had just told the story of "Adam and Sex."

I sincerely apologized. Aicha understood and was gracious and forgiving of my linguistic mistake.

Hesitantly, I started the story again. This time, I said, "Adam and his wife." That is the same story I always tell in Arabic. In fact, I think I have forgotten Adam's wife's name.

LET'S WEAVE CULTURES!

What language and cultural bloopers have you made? Have you ever said something vulgar—accidentally?! How did you find out and how did you handle the shock? Tell us your funny (and "not so funny") stories.

About the Author

Dear Reader, if you liked this book, would you please leave a review on Amazon and Goodreads? It helps other readers find the book and get some good language learning laughs. Thank you for your support!

Marci, along with her French husband, four boys, and dog, Samy, is a global nomad, who has traveled to more than thirty countries and has lived in the United States, France, Morocco, and Spain. She is a French and English teacher, certified life coach, and an Arabic translator in government-run safe houses in Spain. She and her husband work among refugees and immigrants. Marci loves to travel, speak foreign languages, experience different cultures, eat ethnic foods, meet people from faraway lands, and of course, tell stories. She also loves giraffes, Dr. Pepper, french fries, and naps!

Sign up for Marci's newsletter by scanning the QR code below or visiting her website—The Cultural Story-Weaver— www.culturalstoryweaver.com:

SCAN ME

More Books by the Author

Discover Marci's other children's books—encouraging children around the globe to explore the great, big world.

The Boy Who Weaves the World

The Boy of Many Colors

Mommy, What's a Safe House?

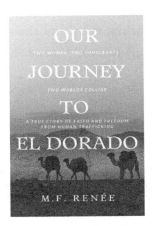

Marci is also the author of . . .

Our Journey to El Dorado—Two Women, Two Immigrants, Two Worlds Collide —A True Story of Faith & Freedom from Human Trafficking.

An unexpected encounter changes the lives of two women—both immigrants searching for purpose and a better life. Through their interwoven journey, both will question and embrace their faith.

When one is asked to be the Arabic translator for a Moroccan woman newly arrived at a Spanish safe house, she has no idea of the journey upon which she is embarking. Born into privilege, she will come face to face with the ugly, dark side of the world, the suffering so many endure. She will also discover the joy and heartbreak of loving broken women, joining forces with them, fighting back to survive and thrive.

Faith will guide their way, faltering at times, returning stronger.

Journey along with them in this sometimes heart-wrenching, sometimes soaring memoir of discovery, disappointment, and redemption.

"M.F. Renée is a poet, and this is a beautiful, powerful story. Her passion for the subject and her friend drips off every page. I'm never going to look at strawberries the same way again." —Lorraine Thomas

"A haunting story to remind us of the horrors some live through in this life . . . but also a beautiful story to remind us there is hope and redemption." —Kat Caldwell

"While the subject matter is difficult, the story is not. It is a lovely tale of friendship, faith, and the difference even one person can make in the world. Read it, and share it." — Madison Michael

—ελε—

Find Marci's books by scanning the following QR code or visiting her website, www.culturalstoryweaver.com:

SCAN ME

Connect With Marci

The Cultural Story-Weaver—Stories to Cultivate Cultural Awareness, Understanding, and Appreciation

www.culturalstoryweaver.com

Facebook: https://www.facebook.com/culturalstoryweaver

Instagram: https://www.instagram.com/culturalstoryweaver/

Twitter: https://twitter.com/culturalstory

LinkedIn: https://www.linkedin.com/in/the-cultural-story-weaver/

Pinterest: https://www.pinterest.com/culturalstoryweaver/

Sign up for Marci's newsletter, "Let's Weave Cultures":

SCAN ME

Made in the USA
Middletown, DE
08 November 2021

51722581R10086